MW01003052

Sign of Life

❧ Sign of Life ❧

A Story of Family,
Tragedy,
Music, and Healing

Hilary Williams
with M.B. Roberts

DA CAPO PRESS
A Member of the Perseus Books Group

*This book is dedicated to
my amazing, loving family and to all the
wonderful people who literally saved my life.
I am also so grateful for the encouragement of
all those who made this book possible, especially
my agent, Sharlene Martin, my editor,
Ben Schafer, and everyone at Da Capo Press.
I thank you from the bottom of my heart.*

Designed by Brent Wilcox

Set in 11.5 point Garamond Pro by The Perseus Books Group

Library of Congress Cataloging-in-Publication Data
Williams, Hilary, 1979–
  Sign of life : a story of family, tragedy, music, and healing / by Hilary Williams with M.B. Roberts.
    p. cm.
  ISBN: 978-0-306-81913-1 (hardcover : alk. paper)
  1. Williams, Hilary, 1979– 2. Singers—United States—Biography. 3. Country musicians—United States—Biography. I. Roberts, M.B. (Mary Beth) II. Title.
  ML420.W5505A3 2010
  782.421642092—dc22
  [B]
                                                                                                    2010026009

Published by Da Capo Press
A Member of the Perseus Books Group
www.dacapopress.com

Da Capo Press books are available at special discounts for bulk purchases in the U.S. by corporations, institutions, and other organizations. For more information, please contact the Special Markets Department at the Perseus Books Group, 2300 Chestnut Street, Suite 200, Philadelphia, PA 19103, or call (800) 810-4145, ext. 5000, or e-mail special.markets@perseusbooks.com.

10 9 8 7 6 5 4 3 2 1

Contents

Foreword

By Hank Williams, Jr.

Every time I look at my daughter Hilary, I see a miracle. I realize every day is a blessing now, more than ever, because she remains with us.

You see, I almost lost my oldest daughter to a car accident in March 2006. For a few precious seconds, we all lost her. Her heart stopped, a result of her blood pressure bottoming out after a one-car accident involving Hilary and her sister, Holly. I won't go into the details; you'll find all that and more in this brave, beautifully written book.

Here's what I'll never forget about that day: Shortly after arriving at the Memphis hospital, I heard the words, "We'll know in the next hour if she's going to make it." I hear those words like it was yesterday. They still bring me to my knees.

Today, as I write this, I'm enjoying my favorite kind of day. I'm at my cabin at Kentucky Lake. My two youngest, Katie and Sam, both pulled in a boatload of croppie fish today. The sun was shining, the fish were biting, my kids were smiling. Let me tell you, it don't get much better than that for ol' Bocephus.

While here, my daughter Holly called, talking about finishing a two-month concert tour that took her to Europe, where I know they fell in love with her, just as everybody does. Hilary called to talk about finishing her book, about her photo shoot for the cover, about her songwriting and recording sessions. I can't wait to hear her new songs. The world better watch out: Hilary may be the quietest and most reserved of my children, but she can also be the most willful and determined. Nothing stops her once she's set her mind to something. She sings like a queen, like a star. My friend Bobby (I never call him Kid Rock, but he doesn't mind if you do) once said, "Man, she's got the bellows!" Ain't that the truth. Good God Almighty, she's got one powerful voice. Just wait until you hear her.

Here's the thing: Hilary is the strongest person I've ever known. People think her Daddy is tough? No, nothing like my daughter. I've had my own miracle and recovery from an accident that should have killed me. But what my daughter has faced, what she's endured and overcome and conquered, well . . . just read this book. You'll see it. Her strength will amaze you and inspire you, as it has all of us who love her.

That strength comes from her faith. Not many people realize how important my faith is to me. It is, and it's been confirmed in the last few years when my prayers to save my beautiful daughter were answered. My prayers joined those of her mother, Becky, sister, Holly, and thousands of others, and I know for certain that is among the reasons Hilary still walks this earth—a bit shaky at times, perhaps, but she gets stronger every day. Like I said, she's one determined young woman. There were those who wondered if she'd ever walk again without a cane. But those of us who know her best always knew she would.

Many of you will know I faced a similar trial at about the same age Hilary has gone through hers. I was twenty-six when I fell five hundred feet down Ajax Mountain in Montana. I underwent thirteen surgeries, or something around there, to build back my face and, well, to save my life. It was touch-and-go there for a while.

Hilary has gone through much more. She's had, what, twenty-three, twenty-four surgeries now? I lose count. Some of them were excruciatingly painful. As bad as it's all been, it was the first day, then the first week, then the first month, then the first several months that stand out. It was bad news on top of bad news. My girl was broken apart, and on top of that, she's diabetic, so there were constant concerns with her blood sugar and with her ability to heal properly. My God, what she went through.

People think once the nurses revived her on the Life Flight helicopter, once she reached the hospital and had expert doctors and specialists caring for her, that she was past the death-defying part. No sir, not even close. Hilary nearly died on us over and over. Each day seemed to bring a new ordeal, as she went from one traumatic surgery to the next. I tell you, we prayed like we've never prayed before, all of us. And here she is, as beautiful and as full of life as ever.

One moment always stands out. She was lying in her hospital bed, so badly injured she couldn't speak. She motioned me over and moved her hands as if playing a fiddle. It took me a few minutes to figure out what she wanted, until she wrote down on a pad, "Mr. Weatherman," the title of one of my songs. She was asking me to sing for her. I've never sang anything with as much feeling as I did that song.

Today, Hilary is the calmest, most together, most spiritual person I know. I'm the proudest papa on earth, that's for damn sure. I know more than ever that the trivial parts of life don't mean a thing. It's a smile from your child. It's a call or a text in the middle of the day. It's hearing someone say "Daddy" in the sweetest tone imaginable.

Let me tell you one more thing: My daughters were spared for a reason. They have been given more time on earth because God has plans for them. I felt the same thing when I didn't die at age twenty-six: God had something for me to do, and I've spent every year since then fulfilling that destiny. With this book, Hilary begins to fulfill hers. It's only the beginning. . . .

Chapter 1

Mississippi Road

As far as the weather goes, the middle of March in Tennessee can go either way. It might be gray, gloomy, and wet, like it had been for weeks, or it could be warm, sunny, and bright green. That particular Wednesday it was perfect: seventy degrees and sunny.

Two days earlier, our mom's father, Warren White, or "Papaw," as we called him, had died at age eighty-six. So my sister, Holly, and I were on our way from Nashville to his funeral in Mer Rouge, Louisiana.

It's tough to put into words just how much Papaw meant to us. The best memories of our life—mine and Holly's—were at Papaw and Granny's beautiful, grand old farmhouse in Mer Rouge, where Mom grew up. We spent lots of traditional Southern holidays there with tables full of food and lots of people and kids running around everywhere. At Christmastime, Papaw would put up the tallest Christmas tree you could imagine, then he would pass out presents to all the grandchildren and cousins and second cousins. In the fall, he'd give us a dollar for picking pecans, and we'd run outside and pick up as many as we could from the ground and put them in little bags.

Every time we visited, we'd go riding in Papaw's gold Jeep Cherokee down these country roads. He had that car forever. It must have had 300,000 miles on it. When I was really little, he would sit me in his lap and let me steer while he pressed down on the pedals with his feet.

Then we'd drive the three miles from his house past the cotton fields and head "downtown." He would walk into the diner wearing his cowboy hat and boots, and he would talk to every single person while I tried to hide behind him, clinging to his leg.

Papaw was a hardworking farmer for most of his life. He also fought in World War II—he was based in Okinawa—and although he hardly ever talked about it, a few years ago, Holly asked him what it was like. All he said was that he saw things a man should never have to see.

Besides working the farm, Papaw did many different things. He raised money to build the local nursing home, and for years, he was head of the Boy Scouts. He was also a really talented artist who was known for his scrimshaw—those intricate carvings made on pieces of whale bone. He sold a lot of his pieces and even made a bolo for George H. W. Bush.

Papaw and Granny both grew up in Mer Rouge; they knew each other since they were kids. He finally asked her out a year or two after he came back from the war. When he died, they had been married over fifty years.

When we got the news that Papaw died, I felt incredibly sad, but the truth was that we'd lost him long ago. He'd been suffering from both Parkinson's and Alzheimer's disease for several years. Our whole family struggled as we watched this noble man slowly decline.

Toward the end, he didn't know who I was. Still, to lose him left this big, empty space, and I felt so bad for Mom. But she told us she had let him go already; the last time she visited, she actually told him goodbye. Nonetheless, she ended up being there when he died. She sat with him and watched him as his breathing got shallower and shallower, and she told him, "Go on, Daddy . . ." It was very peaceful.

So Holly and I were making the seven-and-a half-hour drive to Mer Rouge. I wanted to fly, and my dad even offered to fly Holly and me down in his private jet, but Holly is terrified of small planes. Plus, Dad planned to leave the funeral right when it was over—he was going hunting in Alabama—and Holly and I wanted to stay and visit with the family at least overnight. So we decided to drive.

I know Holly wanted to drive—she likes to be in control—but when I picked her up and didn't offer to move over, she didn't say anything. I guess she figured she already got her way and didn't want to start an argument.

Holly knew I was in no mood for a fight. I'm usually the most laid-back and chill person you could meet, but the night before we left, I had this major anxiety attack. I can't explain it; I just had this sense of dread.

It actually started the day before the trip. My friend Rhett and I were minding the store at Bamboo, the boutique in Green Hills where I was working, and I kept telling him over and over, "I don't want to go on this trip, Rhett." I must have said it a dozen times. It wasn't like me to obsess about something or to freak out like that, and I know I was bugging Rhett.

"Jeez, Hilary!" he said. "I drive nine hours to go home to Oklahoma all the time. Calm down!"

That night, I was still feeling anxious. My hands were literally shaking as I sent a text to Chris Coleman, Holly's now-husband, saying, "I'm having really bad anxiety. Please pray for me."

I felt a little bit calmer the next morning, but it was weird; when I left the house, I remember closing the door to my bedroom and thinking, "I'm not going to be back for a while . . . "

But what was I going to do? Not go to my grandfather's funeral? That wasn't an option. So we got in the truck, my white Toyota 4-Runner, with me driving and Holly in the passenger seat. Soon, the gorgeous day lightened the mood. We rolled down the windows and headed down the road.

A couple of hours into our trip, just past Tunica, Mississippi, we made a pit stop at an Exxon to get gas, hit the ladies' room, and buy some chips and Diet Cokes. When we got back in the truck, Holly leaned way back in her passenger seat, closed her eyes, and put her feet up on the dashboard. Then she stretched out and stuck her long legs out the window, which was rolled halfway down.

"Do you have to do that, Holly?" I asked. "Can you not sit like a normal person? Holly, please put your seatbelt on!"

"No!" she said, with her eyes still closed. "I don't want to."

"Please?" I said.

She didn't answer me, but she sighed, sat up, and folded her legs back into the truck. As soon as she buckled up, I pulled back onto the road—rustic Highway 61—and we were on our way. Despite its bumps and cracks—or maybe because of them— Highway 61 is known as "The Blues Highway" and has inspired more than a few musical myths and legends. Bob Dylan named his influential 1965 album "Highway 61 Revisited," and legendary blues singer Robert Johnson supposedly sold his soul to the devil in exchange for his talent at a famous "crossroads," believed by many to be the junction of Highway 61 and Highway 49 in Clarksdale, Mississippi.

Truthfully, I wasn't thinking about myths and legends at that moment. We still had a long way to go down this mostly two-lane road, and I was thinking we needed some new music. I had just talked on the phone to a friend of mine back in Nashville, Tony Armani, so I grabbed the iPod and put on Patty Griffin's album *Flaming Red* and punched up the song *Tony*, which is a great song but actually kind of depressing because it's about a gay guy who kills himself. There's a line in there that says, "I think I might do a little dying today . . . "

I decided to change the song, so I reached down for my iPod, just for a second. Then, I felt the car shift.

Immediately, I put both hands back on the wheel and gripped it hard. The part of the road we were riding on had turned really rough with deep ruts, as if the tires of a huge 18-wheeler had dug into the asphalt when it was wet and no one had come back and paved it over. All at once, my truck was riding in the deep, dipping part of the ruts and it felt like we were riding a wave at 60 mph. Then the truck skidded across the road and into the gravel and I heard a loud scraping sound, like a bulldozer scooping up a messy pile of rocks.

Holly started screaming—I mean, she was screaming bloody murder. I panicked and overcompensated, jerking the wheel back hard the other way. We came back across the road and spun around across the median and something broke—the axle I think—and the truck flipped over, landing on its right side, and skidded to the edge of the field next to the highway.

As we slid, the tire blew or the wheel popped off—I'm not sure which—then we rolled over four times before finally the truck slammed to a stop on its side. Then, everything went silent.

As I hung nearly upside down from my seatbelt, everything went black. I thought I was blind. I was terrified. I could barely breathe, I couldn't see anything, and everything was completely still. I called out for Holly but she didn't answer me. I thought she was dead. Then, a minute or two later, I heard her moaning so I knew she was alive. Thank God! Then she started screaming.

Immediately, my head started spinning. People always say that your life flashes before your eyes when you're hurt really bad and think you're about to die. For me, it happened just that way. A series of vivid flashbacks played in my mind, like clips from old movie reels. Mostly the images were childhood memories: me as a little girl wearing cowboy boots, me playing with a ball, our house in Alabama where we lived when I was a baby. As the images swirled, I kept thinking, "No, stop! I don't want to die! I'm too young. I want to get married. I want to have kids. I want to go to Europe! I don't want to die . . . "

I knew we needed a miracle, so I cried out to God, "You've got to help us! Please send us your angels!"

The timeline is really fuzzy, but the next thing I remember is a man talking to me. It was a sixty-nine-year-old truck driver from Missouri, Walter Isbell, who saw the accident and stopped. He was the first one to reach us. He grabbed my hand and rubbed my arm and said over and over, "You've got to stay awake, sweetheart. C'mon now, don't go to sleep!"

And all I wanted to do was go to sleep. But he kept talking and kept me awake. I said, "Oh my God, my hip's not right . . . "

In fact, my left hip was halfway down my leg.

Mr. Isbell just kept talking in a soothing voice, "It's broken, honey. Just hang in there."

I could tell something was wrong with my ankle, too. I couldn't move far enough to reach down and touch it. I felt nothing except the cushioning of the pale pink Ugg boots I was wearing. It felt strange; I couldn't control any part of my leg.

Soon, several other people stopped and got out of their cars to help, including a physical therapist and his sister along with a preacher and his wife from Greenville, Mississippi. Someone called 911, then the preacher's wife walked over toward the truck and started praying out loud while another woman got out her phone, came toward us, and said, "Girls, I need your mama's phone number . . . "

Holly was really out of it. The sun roof had slammed against her head; it knocked her out for a few minutes and gave her a concussion. She thought she was having a bad dream and kept saying, "Where am I? Somebody wake me up!" When someone told her she had been in a car wreck in Mississippi, she said, "That's impossible! I'm not in Mississippi . . . I live in Nashville!" Then Holly started yelling, "We're Hank Jr.'s daughters!" but I don't think it really registered with anybody. Then somehow Holly remembered Mom was in Louisiana and called out my Aunt Donna's phone number. She tried to, anyway. But she kept saying the number wrong so I spoke up as loudly as I could, " . . . it's 0-1 not 1-0!"

They got through to my aunt's house, where Mom was sitting at the kitchen table talking with Karen, my cousin's wife, who was going to sing at my grandfather's funeral that afternoon. My cousin Sarah Beth answered the call. She took the phone out of the room for a moment, then walked back in and handed the phone to my Uncle Shelby. Then, he left the room for a long time. Mom was sitting there thinking, "Why does everyone keep taking the phone out of the room?"

Finally, Uncle Shelby came in and said to Mom, "Becky, you need to get on the phone with this lady. The girls have been in a wreck, but everything's going to be fine . . . "

Mom took the phone and the woman began explaining what was going on, "There's been a wreck. They're hurt . . . "

The ambulance hadn't arrived yet. There was a lot of commotion, and through the phone receiver, Mom could hear everything going on in the background, including Holly yelling, "Am I dying?"

The woman said, "They're hurt. It's awful. It's really bad . . . "

Mom's eyes went wide and she couldn't speak. Then, the preacher's wife got on the phone. She spoke to Mom for a moment, and then they began to pray together. My mom has a really strong faith, but she's a refined, reserved person—not exactly the weeping and wailing type. But she and this Pentecostal woman on the other end of the phone began praying together, softly at first, and then it escalated to where they both began loudly rebuking the spirit of death in the name of Jesus.

Mom said later that something just took hold of her at that moment. She thought the devil was taking her daughters away from her and it made her furious. The preacher's wife stayed on the phone with her, shouting, "Halleluiah! Jesus is here! Jesus is here! It's going to be all right!"

Hearing what was going on was bad enough, but thank God Mom couldn't see what was happening. Because I was temporarily blinded due to losing so much blood, I couldn't see anything either, but as people described it to me later, Holly looked gory. Her head was swollen up like a pumpkin and was completely covered with glass and blood. The windshield had caved in, all dented and curved inward, with one enormous, jagged piece pointing directly at Holly's head like a big sword. It stopped just an inch from her forehead; it's a miracle her face wasn't shredded.

Holly's right arm was pinned under the truck. At that point, no one could tell if her arm was still attached to her body. God, could she have lost her arm?

I was still hanging by my seatbelt and it was cutting off my air, making it hard to breathe. My breath was getting shallower and shallower, so I called out to the people gathered around the truck, "You've got to push this over!" Then, I'm not sure exactly who did it, but several of those Good Samaritans came together and pushed on the truck until it rolled upright. You'd think it would have slammed down hard when they pushed it over, but I remember it landing softly, like something (or someone?) was guiding us gently down onto the muddy ground.

Incredibly, Holly still had her arm, although it was broken in two places: her wrist and the part above her elbow. Even more amazing was that despite the fact that her arm essentially bore the weight of the crushed vehicle, her bone wasn't shattered.

"My arm is kind of sore," Holly said, which I'm sure gave the people at the scene a brief moment of comic relief. Because Holly admits to being a total chicken when it comes to pain—she cries when she gets her eyebrows waxed—she had to have been in shock. I'm grateful she didn't remember any part of the actual crash and that everything else that happened directly afterward—at least for her—is a total blur.

By that point, I was also in shock. My face was ashen white and my lips were blue. Blood was oozing out of me from all the torn arteries and veins, and my blood pressure was plummeting. I was going in and out of consciousness, so my sense of time and exactly what happened is foggy. I remember at one point someone saying, "We need to pull her out of the car," and the physical therapist saying, "No! We can't move her. It could kill her!"

I don't know if that was true, but one thing I knew for sure was that I couldn't move by myself. I had too many broken bones to count. Both of my legs, my ankle, my back, collarbone, tailbone, pelvis, right femur, and three ribs were all broken. My hips were shattered. I had a ruptured colon and bruised lungs.

The weird thing was, though, that I wasn't in a huge amount of pain except for the fact that my head was pounding like crazy. And I was freaking out because my eyes were open but I couldn't see, although that turned out to be a blessing because I probably would have passed out if I saw my legs all mangled and facing in the wrong direction.

As I lay there crumpled, I heard people praying, and I know that the preacher's wife was holding my hand. I was trying to stay calm, but then I got a searing pain in my stomach and it became really hard to breathe. I found out later that was when my colon ruptured.

After thirty minutes or so, the ambulance arrived and the emergency crew used the Jaws of Life to pry me from the wreckage. The EMTs were wearing masks; they looked liked welders and cut through the car door like it was nothing. Then they pulled me out, laid me onto a spine board, and set me down in the grass a few feet from the mangled truck.

The EMTs were treating me—Holly was still in the truck—when I heard the puttering sound of helicopter blades. It was a Life Flight helicopter arriving from its base in Tunica, Mississippi, to take us to the trauma center at Regional Medical Center, also known as "The Med," in Memphis, some forty-five miles away.

As the helicopter approached the scene of the wreck, the flight crew had very little information. They only knew that there had been a single-car rollover with serious injuries. Later one of the Life Flight nurses, Cindy Parker, told me that when she looked out the window and saw the truck, it was so mangled that she couldn't identify it as an SUV. She thought it was a station wagon or something. She also thought there was no way anyone could have survived.

Someone on the ground directed the helicopter to land a good distance away from the truck because a policeman noticed leaking gas and feared the truck might catch fire. When they landed, Cindy and her partner, Cindy Bailey—"the other Cindy"—ran over to us.

"Who's the most critical here?"

The EMTs pointed to me. They kneeled down next to me, asked me my name, and one nurse checked me from the toes up while the other checked me from the head down. I kept closing my eyes and as they worked, calling to each other, "We've got to do fluids!" They kept saying, "Hilary! Stay with us, now . . ."

Every time I heard my name, I'd open my eyes and try to smile. Although I don't remember this, at one point I actually started laughing a little when Cindy told me her name was Cindy and her partner's name was also Cindy. She said, "See? We're making it easy for you today."

I was so lethargic; I barely had a pulse and evidently I thought this was the funniest thing ever. Cindy and Cindy. Big Cindy and Little Cindy. Like a *Saturday Night Live* skit.

At some point, the EMTs had also pulled Holly out of the truck and were working on her, too. The crew had called another helicopter for her, which flew in from a different base, just a few minutes behind the first one.

The thing was that I wasn't sure if I'd ever make it on "my" helicopter. I'd lost six pints of blood and, as I lay there, my blood pressure dropped to 55/0. I was between stage 2 and stage 3 of hypoglycemic shock. (There are only four stages; stage 4 is irreversible). I was suddenly overcome by panic and the intense feeling that my chest was caving in and about to collapse. It was like being in a pool drowning. "I can't breathe," I whispered, gasping for breath. "I can't breathe . . . "

That's when I lost consciousness. Then, as the paramedics worked to bring me back, I came out of my body, softly and peacefully. Slowly, my spirit lifted, and soon it was as if I was hovering over the scene looking down on the cars and people below. The feeling of panic and all the pain I felt was gone. I was calm as I watched all the activity around the ambulance and the helicopters. I felt completely peaceful, as if I was high on the mellowest of tranquilizing drugs. It was complete peace—the most joyful feeling I have ever known.

An angel took my hand and I looked up and saw this amazing gold mansion that looked like it was trimmed with icing, like an enormous birthday cake. It was sparkling, gleaming, and glittering. I can't begin to describe the vibrant, kaleidoscope colors I saw. It was so crazy.

Then I saw Merle Kilgore, my dad's best friend and manager who passed away the year before. Merle was a hilarious, happy-go-lucky guy who had lived an incredible life. He went from carrying Hank Williams's guitar in the '50s to writing songs, such as

"Ring of Fire" with June Carter Cash, in the '60s to performing with my dad in the '70s and '80s and then later becoming his manager. Dad tells the best Merle stories, like how he used to keep one of those laugh boxes by his desk, those little battery-operated things you'd get at a gift store. When someone called him with a dumb idea, he'd hold the box to the phone receiver and push the button: Ha-ha-ha-ha!

When I saw Merle that day, he looked wonderful—not sickly like he did during the months before he died from lung cancer. Here he was right in front of me, smiling and slapping his leg. Then I saw Johnny and June Carter Cash, my dad's godparents. Johnny was playing the guitar and June was playing the harpsichord. Johnny toured with Dad for years; they were really close. Johnny and I share the same birthday—February 26—and even though I never met him, when I turned ten, he called to sing "Happy Birthday" to me. I remember Mom answering the phone, then calling out, "Hilary, you're wanted on the phone." Then she covered the receiver with her hand and whispered, "It's a man with a really deep voice . . . "

It felt so good to see them; there was such an overwhelming feeling of love. And the music—it was gorgeous! It went beyond the song Johnny and June were playing. There were lots of other people sitting in a big circle, singing songs. It was as if they were part of an enormous symphony, all in harmony.

Despite how happy I felt, I couldn't help but think about the movie *Scrooge* and suspect that I was about to be taken on a tour of my life—except I'd be wearing my pale pink Uggs and a cute outfit instead of an old nightgown and nightcap. I kept trying to talk. Over and over I said, "Hey! I'm here!" But nobody responded to me. I couldn't control anything; it was as if I had let go because a higher power was in charge. But there was no frustration or sense of loss. It felt amazing—so much joy! Everything was just perfect.

While still trying to comprehend what was happening to me, I looked over and was stunned to see my grandparents, Hank and Audrey, slowly walking toward me. Both Hank and Audrey died before I was born (in Grandpa Hank's case, long before I was born). I'd never met them on earth but I recognized them right away. I knew them. They looked really young and beautiful; Hank was wearing a white Nudie suit and Audrey was wearing a blue dress with little white polka dots. They walked up to me with big smiles on their faces, and one by one, they each gave me a long hug. I felt absolutely elated.

Then, Hank put his arm around Audrey and they slowly turned and walked away. As I watched them go, I knew I wouldn't be going with them. Then, as quickly as it lifted, my spirit came back down and I returned to my body.

On the ground, the Life Flight nurses had begun infusing a synthetic blood substitute into my veins. The substance, called PolyHeme, is a chemically modified form of human hemoglobin and was developed from research done on the battlefields in the Vietnam War. Because ambulances can't carry blood because it must be kept cool and typed for each patient, PolyHeme was then being tested as an alternative to use with trauma victims at accident sites.

A patient had to fit certain criteria—you had to be awake, over eighteen, in a trauma situation, and so forth—to be included in the PolyHeme study, and I fit most of them. There's been some controversy surrounding the consent aspect of the trial because trauma victims are in no shape to say whether or not they want to participate in the study, but I have no problem with it. I'm grateful they had that substance available in that particular place on that particular day. I believe it saved my life.

After my pulse returned, I was conscious again and one of the Cindys told me they would be moving me to the helicopter and taking me to the hospital in Memphis. So just five minutes after they began the transfusion, they secured my head to the spine board, lifted me onto their stretcher, and rolled me over to the waiting helicopter.

I couldn't see her, but evidently they put Holly on the other helicopter immediately after that. As they lifted me in and secured me inside, I remember thinking how miserable Holly must have been getting on that helicopter. I mean, my sister hates small planes, so imagine how she was going to feel about this ride!

Just as I suspected, later I found out that as she was being wheeled aboard, Holly asked the EMTs, "Do I have to go on this thing? I really don't want to get in there!"

Later, one of the EMTs told my dad that story and they had a good laugh. Then the guy told him that both his girls were very polite, saying "please" and "thank you" and that while she was being treated, Holly asked him how he was doing and where he was from. Just like a good Southern girl—she didn't forget her manners!

I don't remember much about the twenty-minute flight except that it was warm and noisy, but now I know and appreciate what an incredible thing a Life Flight helicopter is. These aircraft are mini-emergency rooms; they have almost everything an ER has, only in smaller and more compact versions. My blood pressure was easing back up, thanks to the PolyHeme, and Cindy and Cindy kept talking to me, "Only five more minutes . . . hang in there, honey . . . almost there . . . Okay, we're getting ready to land . . ."

When we landed on the roof of the hospital, the trauma team was waiting for us. The workers lowered me down on the stretcher and wheeled me across the rooftop toward the elevator, which would take me to the emergency room.

The minute we made contact with the roof, I was jolted wide awake. There must have been bumps or gravel on that rooftop because as we rolled and bumped along, the jarring pain all over my broken body was excruciating! It was horrendous—like knife stabs. I remember thinking—I couldn't speak—"Could y'all please pick up the stretcher?" I thought I was going to pass out. It was the worst pain I felt that day.

Back in Louisiana, Mom was making calls. After she got the call from the accident site, she stayed on the phone with the preacher's wife for about twenty minutes. When she confirmed we were being taken to Memphis, she hung up the phone and dialed my dad's cell phone. Dad was getting a haircut at a barber shop near his home in Paris, Tennessee, but he picked up right away. "Miss Becky?" he said, in a cheery voice. "What can I do for you?"

My mom could barely talk.

"Hank," she whispered. "My brother needs to speak to you."

She handed the phone to my Uncle Shelby, who, despite his shaking voice, got right to the point. "The girls have been in a wreck," he said, "but everything's going to be all right. They're taking them to Memphis."

"Are you sure?" Dad said. He was confused. He'd just gotten a text from Holly not an hour ago saying, "Can't wait to C U today . . . " Dad climbed out of the barber's chair and took a deep breath. "How bad is it?"

"Everything's going to be all right," Uncle Shelby said, choking back tears.

He figured it was better not to give Dad too much information at that point. Not that they knew much. The goal was just to get him to the hospital as quickly as possible.

So Dad called his pilot and arranged to take off for Memphis immediately. Because when he got the call he was already planning to meet the plane to fly to Louisiana for Papaw's funeral, the pilot was in place and they were able to take off right away.

Sign of Life

During the short, fifteen- to twenty-minute flight from Paris to Memphis, Dad got down on his knees in the back of his King Air jet and prayed. He knew things were bad. Uncle Shelby had been bawling on the phone.

"Everything's okay?" he thought. "Bullshit . . . "

He did his best to prepare himself for what he was going to see. But how do you do that?

He just tried to focus and push down the fear. This was a familiar feeling. He couldn't let himself give into it.

Chapter 2

Memphis

Because Mom was in Louisiana, it would take her at least four hours to drive to Memphis, which was some 225 miles from Mer Rouge. She sprung into action—all nervous energy and adrenaline. Her brother-in-law, my Uncle Johnny, insisted on driving her to Memphis. That way her brother and sisters could stay with my grandmother for Papaw's funeral.

It hadn't even sunk in that she would be missing her own father's funeral until she heard my aunt answer the phone; it was a friend offering condolences. "Thank you," she said. "But he's gone. He's in peace. We need to pray for Hilary and Holly right now."

Mom snapped into survival mode. She went to her friend Molly's house, where she was staying, and picked up the small bag she'd brought with her from Nashville with two changes of clothes. Because she'd just arrived in Louisiana two days before, she never really unpacked.

In less than half an hour, they were on the road. When they got in the car, Mom called the hospital to get an update on our condition. Holly and I had just been brought in, so there was a flurry of activity, and really, there wasn't much to tell yet. Hospital staffers aren't supposed to give out detailed information anyway, even when they are talking to a parent. The only thing the person on the other end of the phone said was, "They are both here and both are in critical condition."

My mom was going crazy. What did that mean—critical condition? What was she going to find when she got to Memphis?

She and Uncle Johnny barely spoke as they drove north on Highway 61, past Montrose and Greenville and Cleveland. Just north of Dundee, Mississippi, they drove past the very spot where Holly and I had been lying by the side of the road just a few hours ago. But Mom didn't know that yet. She just did what she had been doing all day long: She prayed . . . and prayed.

I don't remember much of what happened once I arrived in Memphis. It was all pieced together for me later. As far as I know, while Holly's helicopter was setting down on the roof, Cindy Parker and two people from the trauma team had already shuffled me down to the ER and into the shock trauma room, which is like the MASH unit of the hospital. Then, a whole team of doctors, residents, medical students, respiratory therapists, nurses, and lab techs descended on me and worked furiously to assess quickly the massive damage to my body.

They started IV fluids and oxygen and drew blood, which a technician quickly transported to the lab. Next, the orthopedic surgeons and neurosurgeons were called in and quickly did their assessments. I needed surgery—several surgeries—but first, they had to do a CAT scan to check for trauma to the brain, lungs, ribs, or heart and to see if there was any bleeding in my abdomen, which there was; I had a ruptured colon and a mesenteric artery bleed.

As I was rolled out into the hall en route to the CAT scan room, my dad was standing there. When he saw me, he came over and walked alongside the gurney as they rolled me down the hall. He grabbed my limp hand, which was ice cold; my face was gray and both my hands and feet were blue. When they reached the doorway and started to wheel me in, Dad let go of my hand and stood there for a minute as if he wasn't quite sure what to do. Then he turned around, walked into the waiting room, and slumped down in a chair. Cindy Parker—"Big Cindy"—followed him into the family waiting room, where the hospital chaplain had escorted him when he arrived a few minutes before.

Cindy says that he was wearing dark glasses, so she couldn't see his eyes, but she could tell he was incredibly shaken. She introduced herself and explained what the doctors were currently doing and what had transpired during the flight. "Hilary was alert during the flight," she said. "She'd smile when we said her name. Her blood pressure was extremely low, but we got it back up. It's up now . . . "

Dad appreciates a straightforward person such as Big Cindy, and I know that her competence and kindness comforted him. He also felt reassured by Suzanne Wilson, the nurse who came in to explain the PolyHeme study to him and get his consent for it to continue. Although I had already been given PolyHeme at the accident scene and in fact had already received the maximum amount allowed in the study—six units, which equals twelve liters of fluid, approximately six times what most shock trauma patients get—they needed consent to keep tracking the results.

What a job! It must be brutal to be the one to brief a dad when his daughter might be dying and, by the way, sign these papers please? Which he did.

When the nurses left, Dad walked back outside to call Mom. He wanted to let her know how to find us when she arrived. By that time, the news of the accident was on the wire ("Hank Jr.'s Daughters Near Death after Horrific One-Car Wreck in Mississippi"), and some fans and curiosity seekers, along with a couple of TV news trucks, were starting to gather in front of the hospital. A *National Enquirer* photographer had already tried to sneak into the ER with a fake badge, and another one came in dressed as a plumber. "These are my daughters!" Dad said. "Why can't they just leave us alone?"

To avoid any further problems, the hospital arranged for security and a private entrance for family members and close friends. One of the security people, a woman named Cynthia, was especially great to my family. Dad loved her. She was a force to be reckoned with—no one got by her.

She'd come into the family waiting room and tell everybody all the stuff that was going on outside. There was the man who approached the guard, saying that he grew up with Hank Jr. and another guy swore that he was Hank Jr.'s brother, and Dad doesn't have a brother.

The security people delivered the messages—after all, we were expecting some legitimate visitors. For a while, Dad laughed along with everybody else, but then it started to get to him. "I don't know these people!" he said, shaking his head. "They need to go!"

One of the funniest things was when Kid Rock, or Bobby, as we call him, came to the hospital to visit me and nobody would let him through. He gave his real name to the guard, "Hi, Bob Ritchie to see the Williams family," and they turned him away. Then he pulled out the big guns: "C'mon, man. I'm Kid Rock. They're expecting me."

The security guard thought, "Yeah, right. This is just some long-haired dude in a baseball hat."

Bobby didn't hold a grudge against the security people. In fact, he became friendly with Cynthia. When she told him she'd never been to a concert in her entire life, he surprised her with tickets to his show in Memphis that night.

Dad also brought in his own security guy—we called him Detective Dan—to drive family and visitors back and forth from the hotel. He wore a bulky coat and cracked everyone up by saying,

"Want to see what's under here?" Then he'd flash open his coat and show us his billy club, his pistol, and so forth.

Dan stayed for several weeks, and he never let my mom drive to or from the hospital by herself. This was a great relief to everybody because Mom often left the hospital late at night or arrived way before sunrise, and, let's face it, downtown Memphis isn't always the safest place.

While all the craziness was going on outside and I was being prepped for surgery, the ER doctors were working on Holly. She looked like something out of a horror show, with blood caked in her hair and pieces of glass everywhere. Her head was still swollen up like a basketball and the whites of her eyes were completely red.

Holly was still going in and out of consciousness; she was dizzy from the concussion, and the pain of her broken wrist and arm was beginning to kick in. But when she heard the doctor walk in and say, "Razor! Someone please get me a razor!" she sat bolt upright. "No!" she said. "You cannot shave my head! Please!"

Holly has long, wavy blonde hair down to her butt. I can't imagine her looking like Britney Spears gone bad, but as the doctor explained, there were shards of glass and other debris in her hair and on her scalp. If they didn't remove the glass and clean the cuts, she could get an infection. But Holly can be very persuasive. "Please!" she said. "If you cut off my hair, I will die!"

She and I both had already endured the indignity of the Life Flight nurses cutting off all our clothes, although I know they did their best to keep us covered while they were treating us. But in Holly's case, the cut up and discarded clothes included her very favorite jeans that took forever to find because, like me, she is really tall. She just couldn't be bald, too.

The doctor relented, and the nurses gently and patiently pulled the glass out of her hair and stitched her up piecemeal.

Despite how awful she looked and the fact that she was still kind of out of it, Holly really was in good shape. It was hard to believe though, by looking at her—at first anyway—and when my dad came into her room, he pulled up a chair at her bedside and just started bawling.

"Dad, what's going on?" she asked.

"You've been in a horrible car wreck," he explained.

"Where's Hilary?"

Dad paused.

"Is she dead?" Holly asked.

"No! She's on her way to surgery, honey . . . "

Finally, Mom got to the hospital. My uncle dropped her off at the front door, parked her car in the hospital lot, and went right to the airport in a cab. He said he couldn't bear to see me and Holly in the ER Plus, he was anxious to get back to his family and help them get through the funeral.

When Mom was escorted upstairs, several doctors were with me in my room, so right away, Dad took Mom to Holly's room. When Mom walked in and saw Holly, she gasped and covered her face with her hands. Then she took a long, slow, deep breath. Despite how battered Holly looked, Mom was thrilled to see her sitting up and talking. Up until this point, the only information Mom had was that my sister and I were in critical condition. As she drove from Mer Rouge, she didn't know if she'd find us alive when she got here. So when she saw that Holly was responsive, she was incredibly relieved. When the doctors told her that Holly would be released in a couple of days, she sat down, closed her eyes, tightly clasped her hands together, and whispered, "Thank you, Lord."

A few minutes later, a nurse came in and touched Mom on the shoulder. "You can see Hilary now," she said.

My room was dark and I couldn't see very well because I didn't have my contacts in—at some point someone must have taken them out—but I was awake and I saw Mom when she walked in. She came right to my bedside.

"I'm so sorry," I said.

"Hilary, what are you talking about!" she said. "It was an accident. You didn't do anything wrong."

The funny thing was that Mom told me later that, as she sat there reassuring me, she couldn't shake the feeling that she was the one who had done something wrong. She thought, "I'm a sinner. Did I not pray enough for my children? Could I have done something differently? Should I have made them fly to the funeral? Could I have taken better care of them?"

Rationally, I knew that no one was at fault—not me and certainly not Mom. But I just couldn't help feeling really bad about everything. Mom had to leave Papaw's funeral and drive up to Memphis, not knowing if we were dead or alive. And Dad rushed over here and he was just crying and crying. And Holly—how was she? Where was she? At that point, I hadn't seen her and really didn't know. Was she OK?

My face wasn't bruised and cut like Holly's (I was black and blue and purple everywhere else. And thank goodness no one could see the grisly seat belt mark across my stomach), so that was a relief to my mom. I was wearing a neck brace and a head brace and my eyes were swollen shut. They looked like two little slits. My contacts had gotten all scratched up before they were removed, and it still felt like I had sand and dirt in my eyes. I looked like I had pink eye.

I was breathing on a ventilator, and worst of all, I didn't even really look like myself, mostly because I was really, really swollen all over my body from the trauma of the wreck and the fluids they were pumping into me. I looked like I weighed three hundred pounds! In fact, a few days later, when the swelling came down, one of the nurses came in and took a double take. "Hilary, look at you!" she said. "I had no idea you were this skinny. I thought you were big, like a football player!" Thanks . . . I think? I knew I wouldn't be like that forever, but right then, I felt like a big blob, lying there all big and swollen.

Besides my overall appearance, the most shocking sight for people who walked into my room was my leg. My foot was propped way up, and there were all kinds of metal and steel rods sticking out of my heel, ankle, and shin. The metal actually went through the bones. When I first woke up and noticed all the hardware (how could I not?), I asked the nurse if she could please take those metal things out of my leg. It must have been hard for her not to laugh.

The "metal things" were part of a massive metal device called an external fixator, and it would be in place for a month. I had a compound fracture, so they put it on to stretch the bone apart so they could then realign it. I couldn't move my leg at all, but I wanted so badly to shake that thing off! As bad as it felt, though, it looked even freakier. It was like, beam me up! It looked like I was part of a satellite being launched to the moon.

When Bobby first walked into my room, after he'd sorted out his problem with security, he took one look at my leg and all the tubes and wires I had coming in and out of my body and couldn't hide the shock on his face. "Girl!" he said. "You've got more hookups in you than I have in my studio!"

I grabbed a pillow and pulled it down tight against my stomach because he was cracking me up and it hurt to laugh. It's really painful to laugh when you have broken ribs!

His visit was a bright spot in an otherwise dark day. He held up a Get Well card that all his band members had signed, and he read it aloud to me. He'd brought me flowers, too, but he had to leave them outside. (Flowers aren't permitted in the ICU—too many germs.)

Anyway, later that first night, Dad finally went to the hotel to sleep. He had gotten a couple of rooms for people coming into town at the Peabody Hotel, which wasn't very far away. A couple of my friends—Shanna, who I grew up with, and Melody, my roommate in Nashville—came to see me, although I don't remember it. Melody said she took my hand and said, "Hilary, it's me . . . " and that I raised my arm up and squeezed her hand really tight. And Shanna—I'm glad I don't remember seeing her because she was really upset from the sight of me. She said she almost passed out when she saw my swollen, purple body and all the beeping machines closing in around me.

When they came in, I wasn't awake, and the nurses said they could only go in one at a time, so my friends didn't stay with me long. They visited Holly, who was awake and really happy to see people, and then they went back to the hotel with Mom and spent the night in her room. Then, at 5:00 a.m., Mom and Dad came back because I was scheduled for surgery at 5:30 a.m.

I was in and out of surgery constantly those first few days. The first night, they removed and repaired part of my right colon. They also operated on my left femoral neck fracture (the broken part of my thigh just below the hip joint) and my right distal tibial fracture (my broken shin bone). They also secured my broken right thigh bone so they could operate on it later. The chart actually read, "Place right intratrochanteric subtrochanteric femur fracture in traction." These are words I never thought I'd know!

I can only try to imagine how tedious it was for everybody in the waiting room while all this was going on. The first forty-eight to seventy-two hours are critical for trauma patients, but hours would go by without any news or updates. This wasn't the fault of any of the doctors or nurses; when there was something to say, Dr. Martin Croce, the Med's Chief of Trauma and Critical Care, or one of his nurses, Stephanie Panzer or Suzanne Wilson, would find my parents and explain things really clearly.

But unfortunately, those first couple of days, there just wasn't anything to do but wait. I guess that's why they call it the waiting room.

Melody, who has a short attention span and has to stay busy, needed a task, so she went out to find my Sidekick—my pre-iPhone cell phone. Evidently, they had towed my wrecked truck to Memphis, and somehow she found out exactly where it was parked and brought us some of our stuff, including my phone, my purse, and Holly's purse.

At one point, Mom went downstairs with Detective Dan, who was putting the rest of our stuff they'd collected from the accident site into her car. As she picked up my shoes, Holly's jacket, Holly's computer, the registration papers for the truck—all covered and caked in mud—her heart skipped a beat. She couldn't help but picture us lying by the side of the road, hurt and in pain. "This is bad," she thought. Then she shook her head and snapped into adrenaline mode. "I've got to take care of my daughters."

Mom went back upstairs and began rushing around nonstop, attending to everyone who had arrived, including my sister's boyfriend at the time, Chris Janson; his then-manager, Ryan Harrington; and one of my dad's former managers, Ross Schilling. Ever the gracious hostess, Mom did her best to make everyone as comfortable as possible in that cold waiting room with a couple of chairs, one phone, and bright fluorescent lights. She kept thanking everyone for coming and asking if she could get anyone anything. One of the doctors even walked in, looked over at her, and asked Dad, "Where did you get her?"

Dad just shrugged. "She's the perfect Southern belle."

To other people in the waiting room, Dad seemed mostly upbeat, or maybe it was just nervous energy. Once, after they'd been sitting around for hours, he and Bobby went around and visited other patients in the hospital. Some of them were pretty shocked when, out of the blue, Kid Rock and Hank Jr. walked in!

Then Bobby found out about a boy down the hall with a devastating spinal chord injury who just happened to be a huge Kid Rock fan. I wish I could have seen for myself how that kid brightened up when Bobby came to hang out with him in his room.

Back in the waiting room, Dad kept telling all kinds of stories and kidding around. At one point, he noticed that Chris Janson had walked into an adjacent room to be by himself. Dad got up and looked in the room where Chris was on his knees praying. He turned, looked back at everybody, and said, "What's wrong with that boy? He's in there talking to himself!"

All the Life Flight nurses—the ones who flew with Holly as well as my Cindys—made a point to check in on us those first couple of days. The Cindys actually visited me many times throughout my month-long stay in Memphis, partly because it was their job to follow up, especially regarding the results of the PolyHeme study. They also visited us because they are incredibly caring people who do a job I can't even fathom doing.

The first time Little Cindy came to the waiting room to meet my family, Dad didn't believe she was one of the nurses who saved my life. Cindy Bailey is small (hence the nickname, "Little Cindy") and looks really young for her age. What's more, that day she was wearing casual clothes and a baseball cap. When someone introduced her to Dad, he said, "You can't be a nurse! You look like a fourteen-year-old boy!"

Everybody laughed and Dad gave her a big bear hug. That was a great moment—a welcome break from the hours of stress and worry.

When things quieted down, Dad started telling Cindy about his own life-altering accident, just over thirty-five years ago. His accident was awful: He fell off a mountain in Montana and split open his head, crushed his face, and lost a whole lot of blood. It took over six hours for a helicopter to reach him and take him to the hospital. It's an absolute miracle that he survived.

His recovery, consisting of nine initial surgeries—and a few more down the road—was long and painful, and some things, such as his eyesight, never completely returned to normal. At one point, he took off his hat and showed Cindy his scars. Then, as he talked about the accident, it occurred to him that when he fell off the mountain, he was almost exactly the same age as me; he had been twenty-six, and I had just turned twenty-seven. He knew what I was facing, and thinking about it made his heart sink.

When I woke up after surgery—I'm not sure if it was the first or second one—the first thing I saw in my dark room when I opened my eyes was my dad sitting in a chair next to my bed. He had his eyes closed and his head down and he was holding my hand. I couldn't speak because I had breathing tubes in my nose and down my throat, so I just watched him. His chest was moving up and down and he was breathing heavily. He was crying hard. I just watched him for a long time. And then I closed my eyes and cried a little bit, too.

Sometime during the second day in the hospital—I think it was in the afternoon—Holly came into my room. I was groggy from painkillers, but I perked up right away. Everyone told me Holly was fine, but I just didn't know. My mind was doing crazy things, so I just had to see for myself. I was dying to talk, but I still had all those tubes down my throat, so I started waving my hands around.

"What's wrong?" Holly asked.

I kept motioning.

"What?" she said. "A violin? Music?"

Then I started making a writing motion with my hand.

"Oh!" Holly said. "She wants to write a note."

The nurse handed me a pen and paper, and I scribbled on it, "I'm so happy to see you! I didn't think you were alive . . . "

We both started crying. Holly says she wished she'd saved that note.

For the next week or so, if I wanted to communicate something more complicated than "yes" or "no," I had to write it down. So the nurse gave me one of those boards that I could write on with a dry erase marker and then wipe it off.

One day, my Aunt Jo Lynn came to visit. I was so happy when Mom told me she was on the way. She had stayed in Mer Rouge for my grandfather's funeral, and then, when everyone left, she drove right up to Memphis.

I was sleeping when she got there; I was really out of it from morphine, or maybe by that point, it was another painkiller, probably Dilaudid. But eventually, I opened my eyes and half-smiled at her, so she decided to try to cheer me up. She leaned over close and said, "Guess what, Hilary? I was just talking to your daddy and he said he'd buy you any kind of car you want!"

The drugs had me in a serious fog, so I couldn't write very well, but somehow I managed to pick up the board and write in big, bold letters, M-E-R-C-E-D-E-S . . . C-O-N-V-E-R-T-I-B-L-E. Then, using all the colored markers, I drew a big rainbow over it. Aunt Jo Lynn went to the waiting room to find my dad. "Well, Hank," she said. "The good news is she's awake. The bad news is . . . she wants a Mercedes!"

Dad came bursting in the room, all smiles, when he heard that I was awake. I smiled back at him, and he just laughed and laughed. Aunt Jo Lynn shook her head and said, "If I have to work three jobs, I'm getting her that car!"

The next day, when Dad walked in the room, he was carrying a brochure for the Mercedes ML 350. Okay, it's not a convertible, but it's an awesome SUV with a five-star crash-test rating. It doesn't roll over very easily and has all kinds of safety devices and air bags. He said, "Pick out the color and the interior you want."

I was so excited! I wanted heated seats, but I had to choose between satellite radio and heated seats, so the radio won. He bought it for me that week, complete with a navigation system, and even though I wouldn't be able to drive it for many months—at that moment, I couldn't even fathom getting behind the wheel of a car—it was so great to have something to look forward to.

The wreck happened on a Wednesday. On Friday, I went in for what was probably my third or fourth surgery. It's hard to keep track; I had trauma surgeries and orthopedic surgeries, one after another. But this one was memorable because, for the second time, I almost died.

During the procedure to repair my shattered femur, I went into pulmonary edema, which basically means my lungs, which were badly bruised from the accident, were filling up with fluids. I wasn't getting enough oxygen and my blood pressure plummeted. The surgery was cut short and the doctors put me on life support. For several hours, they feared that I might die, which trumped their earlier fear that they would be forced to amputate my leg in order to save my life.

Earlier, the doctor had told Mom, "We have a very serious situation here, Mrs. Williams. We'll know in the next couple of hours whether we're going to be able to save her. We may have to take her leg. It may come down to life over limb."

I don't think Mom realized how serious it was—or maybe she wanted so badly to believe that it wasn't very serious—until after the surgery when I was back in my room. She peeked through a curtain to see what was happening and saw a dozen people— doctors, nurses, and the CEO of the hospital—all gathered around my bed. As Dad remembers, "There was gray hair all the way around her bed."

A nurse came out and told her, "Ma'am, she's in pretty bad shape. Right now we're just watching her."

Mom walked into the room and Dad was there, again at my bedside, crying uncontrollably. Mom said she didn't cry. She wouldn't cry. According to her, God gave her an inner strength. She was determined to hold it together for everyone, especially Holly. She went into Holly's room and Holly kept asking her, "What's going on with Hilary?"

"Everything's going to be fine," Mom told her, as she busied herself propping up Holly's pillows and smoothing her blanket. Looking at Mom, Holly could believe it.

Then Mom walked out into the hall and found a small room next to the nurse's station where she could be alone. She prayed out loud to God, "Lord, this is really hard because I know Hilary could die. You know her future. If her future would be so terrible, then take her. Your will be done. I want her to stay here, but I put it in your hands."

By early evening, my heart rate was down and my blood pressure had crept back up. My condition was stable and I was sleeping soundly.

As she did many times over the next few months, Mom recited a Bible verse out loud to me from Isaiah 40:28–29:

Have you not known? Have you not heard? The everlasting God, the Lord, the Creator of the ends of the earth, does not faint or grow weary; there is no searching of His understanding. He gives power to the faint and weary, and to him who has no might He increases strength (causing it to multiply and making it to abound) . . .

She also read from Isaiah 43:2:

When you pass through the waters, I will be with you, and through the rivers, they will not overwhelm you. When you walk through the fire, you will not be burned or scorched, nor will the flame kindle upon you.

That night, when Mom went back to the hotel room, she was all alone. My friends had gone home. It was too late to make any phone calls. So she sat there by herself. And finally, she cried. She cried for a long time.

Chapter 3

Falling

In the summer of 1975, my dad was twenty-six years old and found himself at a major crossroads in his career and life. He'd been performing professionally since he was eight years old, mostly singing my grandfather's songs. Then, when he was a teenager, in addition to his young Hank Williams act, he sometimes hit the stage as "Rockin' Randall," when he sang and played drums, electric guitar, and boogie-woogie piano in his own rock-and-roll band. By the time he reached his mid-twenties, the musical schizophrenia in addition to the grind of the road and drama in his personal life had definitely taken its toll.

For the preceding few years, Dad was living a life of extremes. He'd ride the high of a number-one hit, and then follow that up with drinking binges and fights with his then-wife, Gwen. He'd perform a fantastic show, then cap it off with another drug-and-alcohol binge and a series of no-shows—and, of course, more fights with Gwen. He'd buy a new car, wreck it after a night of partying, and leave it by the side of the road. This was one tormented guy.

More than anything, Dad wanted desperately to stop riding his father's coattails and to develop his unique personal musical style, but he was constantly discouraged from doing so by his record company and especially his mother, my grandmother

Audrey. There was just too much money to be made as a Hank Williams clone.

Fans discouraged him, too. If he sang his own songs or slipped into his own interpretation of "Long Gone Lonesome Blues," fans would often boo or get up and leave. He'd even had fans spit on him.

The pressure was closing in from all directions. Then, one night in 1974, feeling frustrated, depressed, and desperate, Dad swallowed an entire bottle of Darvon pain pills while he was home alone in Cullman, Alabama. A handyman found him the next morning and called his good friend and manager, J. R. Smith, who rushed him to the hospital.

He'd hit rock bottom. And when you hit rock bottom—at least when a guy like my dad does—you stop worrying about everything you might lose and start following what's in your heart. For Dad, that meant music. And the music that stirred him most during the early '70s was the Southern rock of bands such as Lynyrd Skynyrd, Charlie Daniels, Marshall Tucker, and the Allman Brothers.

Dad's vision was to marry country music, which he loved, with this innovative new sound that young, rock-influenced audiences were embracing. So when it came time to make his next record in early 1975, he headed south, away from Nashville and straight to the hotbed of Southern rock—Muscle Shoals, Alabama.

He recruited some great players to join him at Music Mill Studios that February, including the Allman Brothers' Dickey Betts and Chuck Leavell, the Marshall Tucker Band's Toy Caldwell, and Charlie Daniels, who contributed his part on tape. The result, which they finished in July, was *Hank Jr. and Friends*, the album that would define the rest of my dad's career.

Now, he just had to wait a month or so until he could debut his new music. But waiting is not something my father does very well.

He was feeling restless. His divorce from Gwen was in the works, and he had several weeks before the new tour kicked off in September. So he stayed busy by taking flying lessons. Then he made plans to visit his friend Dick Willey in Montana, where they could hike and he could get in shape for the tour as well as for a Canadian Rockies hunting trip he planned to take later that fall.

The week before Dad was due to leave for Montana, he drove up to Nashville to buy an airplane. Even buying the plane didn't cure his restlessness—a fact that didn't escape the dealer, his old friend Campbell Lauther, who said, "I have an idea, Hank. I'm going to fix you up with a girl."

Dad was sitting in Campbell's office, looking at pictures on his desk. He picked up a photo of a softball team and pointed to a pretty girl in the front row. She was wearing a baseball cap and a warm, friendly smile. "Okay," Dad said. "How about this girl?"

"You wouldn't like her," Campbell said. "She's not . . . wild."

But Dad was insistent. "It's her or nothing," he said.

So Campbell Lauther called the girl in the picture, Becky White, who worked as a receptionist at ABC Dot Records. He asked her if she was busy that night. When she said she wasn't, he handed the phone to Dad. "Hello, Becky?" Dad said. "This is Hank Williams, Jr., and you don't know me, but I just bought an airplane and I'm broke. Could you take me out to dinner tonight?"

Well, Becky, who was—and is—a good, conservative, properly raised Southern girl (and just happens to be my mom), decided it would be alright to go out—just for supper. When she hung up the phone, Mom turned to her friend Charlotte Tucker and said, "Who's Hank Williams, Jr.?"

Charlotte could not believe my mom had worked in the country music business for over a year and didn't know who Hank Jr. was. Mom graduated two years before with a music degree from LSU, but growing up, she mostly listened to pop music like Ricky

Nelson or the Beatles. She knew who Hank Sr. was, though. And she remembered going to the 1964 movie *Your Cheatin' Heart*, which starred George Hamilton as Hank Williams, and crying her eyes out. Despite the fact that fourteen-year-old Hank Jr. sang all the songs on the soundtrack of the movie that had made her bawl, she was unfamiliar with the icon's son. In retrospect, this was probably a very good thing.

Her friend warned her that Hank Williams, Jr., was crazy, had been married "a bunch of times," and that she shouldn't go out with him. But Mom had already accepted his invitation ("He was so sweet on the phone," she said), and besides, they were going out in a group.

So my parents went to dinner that night, joined by Dad's dear friend Merle Kilgore and Dad's hunting buddy, Bill Dyer, and his wife. After dinner, the five of them went to see the movie *Jaws*. My dad took Mom home, and according to him, they talked and talked forever. Then he kissed her goodnight.

They went out a couple more times that week. Their dates were pretty tame. Mostly they went out to eat and talked and held hands. But one night, Dad had a lot to drink and danced on the table at the restaurant. Mom, who didn't really drink much, thought this guy might be too wild for her. Then, the night before he left for his trip, he said, "I love you, Becky."

Mom says she told him, "Well, Hank. I like you a lot, but . . . "

Then he left for Montana.

My dad is most at home and at peace when he's hunting, fishing, or roaming around a field searching for Civil War relics. Holly always says, "Ask him about music, and he won't say much. But ask him about the buck he shot? He'll never shut up."

For most outdoorsmen, the actual hunting or fishing part is secondary. It's the stillness and the quiet and the closer-to-God aspect of being outside and experiencing nature that Dad truly loves. Given the spectacular, God's-country scenery of Montana, it's easy to understand why he chooses that particular place to revive.

That week in August of 1975, he and Dick Willey, along with Dick's eleven-year-old son, Walt, were hiking high in the Bitterroot Mountains, right along the edge of the Continental Divide. When they looked down, they were standing in Montana, but they could see the village of Salmon, Idaho, way down in the valley below. The air was thin at 11,000 feet, so they stopped to catch their breath before making their way up and around Ajax Mountain.

Even in August, the peaks of Ajax were covered with snow. Dad says there's probably been snow on that mountain since the beginning of creation. And it's the snow you have to watch out for; a soft blanket of snow could be deceiving. What looked solid and quiet and innocent could be covering up something treacherous. Indeed, that turned out to be the case that day.

After Dick and Walt made their way across a snow field, Dad started after them. He was nearly halfway across the field, slowly and carefully following their trail and crunching the snow with each step, when a rock shifted under his right leg. Then, the ground began to drop under his left leg. As the mountain shifted and the snow slid, he fell headfirst and plunged down the side of the mountain.

Dad has described these next terrible moments of his life many times. It sickens me to imagine it, and I can't help noticing certain similarities between his accident and my car wreck. As he fell, he felt rocks cutting him, slashing his arms, hands, and legs. The rocks were slicing his face and the snow was burning his eyes, but at that point, it didn't really hurt—not yet.

I knew that feeling: Shock. Disbelief. A surreal swirling. A pain that would set in soon enough.

He desperately tried to right himself and even managed to curve around at one point so he was sliding feet first. But he was helpless, and even though he desperately tried to dig in his hands or feet or grab onto something, he kept sliding and tumbling down. Then, from high above him, he heard Dick and Walt's piercing screams as he slammed face first into an enormous boulder.

Dad's first thought as he lay there slumped by the jagged gray rock was that he was okay. He looked down at his bloody and scraped-up hands and thought, "They're there! I still have my hands. I'm all right."

Meanwhile, Dick was half-running and half-sliding to reach Dad. I try not to think about what Dick and poor little Walt, who came along a few minutes behind his father, saw when they reached him. Dad could see the horrified, stunned look on Dick's face. But Dick kept his composure. "It's not as bad as you think, Hank," he said. "Your nose is broken . . . "

But Walt couldn't help himself. He screamed when he saw my father, whose head and face were shattered. Dad's nose was gone, one eye was hanging down, and when he reached up to touch his mouth, his teeth and parts of his jaw fell into his hand. The worst of it was that Dad's brain was exposed, protruding slightly from his forehead.

Dick snapped into action. He laid Dad down in the snow and, while cradling his head with one hand, used the other to reach in and push his brain back into position. He collected the broken pieces of my father's skull and then took off his own shirt and wrapped it around Dad's head.

Dick knew that if Dad had any chance of survival, he had to go for help. There were no cell phones back then, so he'd have to make his way down the mountain—a long way—and, somehow, return with help. And Walt would have to stay with Dad to watch him, talk to him, and keep him awake.

Imagine being a father in that position. Your friend will die if you don't leave your eleven-year-old boy with him. What if Dad died? Dick would have to live with the fact that he'd left his boy alone on the mountain with a dead body. What a choice.

Walt stayed and talked to Dad for several hours. He rattled on about hunting and fishing and his old coon dog. It was just like the truck driver who talked to me, held my hand, and kept me awake after my car wreck. He saved me. And Walt saved my dad.

It breaks my heart to picture Walt sitting there in the cold with Dad as the sun started going down. Dad said he remembered at one point looking over and seeing tears rolling down Walt's face. Then, finally, they both heard Dick calling for them.

Although it seemed like forever to Walt and Dad, Dick probably broke a land-speed record getting down the mountain and back to them. He'd basically run down the mountain to where his Jeep was parked, got in, and sped dangerously down the rough, rugged logging trail. Halfway back to his cabin, he smashed into the side of a bridge and drove into a creek. He shifted into four-wheel drive and, incredibly, the Jeep made it up the almost vertical incline and was back on the road. Dick was still ten miles away from his cabin and what he thought was the closest phone when, to his amazement, he spotted a Forest Service vehicle.

Dad says you could go months without seeing a Forest Service vehicle in that area, and there was a ranger just sitting there, as if he was waiting for Dick. After the ranger called for a helicopter, Dick made his way back up the mountain to Walt and Dad.

It was then when Dad really started to feel the pain and the chill. I think of how cold he must have been, lying on the mountain. The cold turned out to be a blessing, though. The doctors later said that it prevented infection and helped save him. Even so, it must have been a painful, piercing cold.

When the helicopter arrived, the pilot landed on the closest piece of flat land, some two hundred feet away. The medic hopped out and bounded over to him with a stretcher. They lifted Dad up and strapped him onto it, and after twenty minutes of agony—bumping up and down rocks to get to the helicopter— they fastened the stretcher, with Dad still in it, to the outside.

He screamed and struggled as the helicopter took off and transported him to a nearby ranch with a landing strip. Again, I think of the cold and the noise and how scared he must have been riding on the outside of a helicopter. I think if he could have broken the straps and just fallen off, he would have.

He was transferred to a small plane at the ranch, which flew him a hundred miles to Missoula. After another short helicopter ride, this time on the inside, he was finally at Community Hospital. It had been eight hours since his fall.

Back in Nashville, my mom was sitting by the pool at her apartment building when her friend Charlotte came over. "Have you heard the radio?" Charlotte said. "Hank fell off a mountain in Montana. He's in critical condition!"

Mom couldn't believe it. She didn't know what to think. She'd just met this guy two weeks ago. They had a couple of dates, the last one just a week before. And now . . .

Evidently, Dad had already told people about "the girl he met in Nashville," because that night his mother called Mom and asked her to come to Montana. Now Mom really didn't know what to think.

Then, Dick Willey called Mom and told her it probably wasn't a good idea for her to come. At that point, Dad was really fighting for his life. It was day two, and the doctors said he would be out of the woods if he lived for eight days. Gwen was at the hospital, along with lots of other people. Mom agreed. She didn't think it was appropriate for her to go. But she felt awful and worried and wanted to do something. Dick told her, "Just keep calling Hank." Dad had told him all about Mom, so Dick knew it would lift his spirits to hear from her.

She did call a few times and wrote some letters, but my mom says she really didn't know if she would ever see him again. He never said, "See you soon," or "I'll call you when I'm in Nashville." He was being completely noncommittal. The truth is that Dad was severely depressed. He thought he'd never sing again and told Dick that his love life was over. Who could love somebody with no future, not to mention someone with a horribly mangled face?

After spending two weeks in the hospital, Dad moved in with Dick Willey and his wife, Betty, at their home in Polson, Montana, for a while. I know it was a tough time for him, especially because his jaws were wired shut and he couldn't eat. But it cracks me up when he describes the "health shakes" Betty made for him. They were packed with vitamins and nutrients, but they were lime green and didn't taste very good. (Dick called them "Puke Shakes.")

Dad dreamed of eating solid food. For some reason, he kept picturing the perfect tuna fish sandwich, and when the doctors removed the wires from his jaw, he raced back to Dick and Betty's, grabbed a can of tuna out of the cupboard and made one right away. At first, he forgot he didn't have any teeth and got really frustrated and mad when he couldn't take a bite out of the sandwich. But Betty cut it up for him into tiny pieces and it tasted magnificent.

In October, Dad went home to Alabama. He made several trips up to Nashville, usually for physical therapy sessions at his friend Christine Longyear's house or at her salon near Music Row. After one of these sessions, Christine came into the room where he was resting after the session and said, "Hank, Becky's here . . ."

My dad says he was furious. He was mortified about the way he looked, and he knew that Christine had set this up despite the fact that he told her he didn't want to see anyone, especially Mom.

The day before, Christine had called Mom (they had become friends, too) and convinced her to come over even though Dad had asked her not to. Mom was hesitant. She's not the pushy type, and it's very unlike her to go where she's not invited. But Christine convinced her that Dad really wanted and needed to see her and that it was truly meant to be. And it was.

When Dad walked into the room and saw Mom, he lit up. He says that when he looked at her, she was so beautiful and smiling, but the best part was that he saw no shock or revulsion on her face. Obviously, Mom thought Dad looked different. She could see that his teeth were knocked out and his eye was kind of messed up, but she says she didn't really look at his scars. "I had a lot of compassion, like anybody would," she said. "I just felt so bad for him. I saw his heart. He had such a sweet heart."

So they started seeing each other. Dad's spirits were high, and a week or two later, he drove to Nashville where his dentist was due to fit him with nine new teeth. He was sitting in the chair with his mouth wide open when the dentist broke the bad news: His upper and lower jaws were not lined up properly. He couldn't replace his teeth until his jaws were rebroken, rewired, and made to heal correctly.

Dad was crushed. Getting his jaws rebroken, even in a doctor's office, was hideous. And rewiring them shut? Again? That was—literally—tough to swallow.

To cheer him up, my mom invited him to come home to her parents' house in Mer Rouge, Louisiana, for Thanksgiving. I laugh when I think of Mom picking him up in her tiny little stick-shift Mercury Capri, with no radio, no air conditioning—it's still hot in Louisiana in November—and driving him seven-and-a-half hours from Nashville to Mer Rouge. Here was this big guy who was used to riding around in Cadillacs now saying, "No, no! This is fine . . ."

My grandparents' house was a big, beautiful Southern farm house, complete with pecan trees in front and horses out back. At holidays, there were always loads of people there, and that Thanksgiving was no exception.

It was hard for Dad to talk because he had stitches on the roof of his mouth, and, obviously, it was also impossible for him to eat solid food. So as he sat watching everyone devour turkey and dressing and potatoes and pumpkin pie, he sipped through a straw a Thanksgiving "shake" that my grandmother June, who we later called "Granny," made for him. Granny actually put one of everything from the Thanksgiving table in a blender—from turkey to cranberries—and chopped and blended it until it was smooth enough to pour. And he drank every bit of it.

Dad and Mom were definitely falling in love. But that weekend Dad also formed a deep bond with my grandfather Warren, a hard-working, no-nonsense farmer, hunter, and fisherman who, with his cowboy hat and boots, was just my father's kind of guy. Papaw and Dad were instant friends. Over the years, they fished and hunted together and, most importantly, even after my parents got divorced, they loved each other until the day Papaw died.

My mom had a very stable, very traditional, small-town Southern upbringing that was rounded out by a supportive, loving extended family. I think that was one of the things that attracted my dad to my mom; this was so different than what he had known, and, for a while anyway, he embraced it.

The warmth of Mom's family home probably felt especially welcoming to my dad that first Thanksgiving because, just a few weeks earlier, his mother Audrey had passed away at the age of fifty-two.

Dad loved his mother. Even though they were professionally and personally estranged at the time, Audrey flew to Montana to be with Dad after his mountain fall. People tell me that she was completely devastated. Just three months later, she died. She had a lot of financial and personal problems at the time of her death, and it pains me to know that she died thinking that Dad's life was in ruins.

Dad keeps a lot of his feelings inside, so he didn't talk about his mother much after her death. But these days, he brings her up now and again, and when he speaks about her, it's usually with great reverence. He has pointed out to me and Holly a number of times that Audrey Williams played many more shows than Hank Williams ever did, which is true. She put together dozens of tours and often performed, both before and after Hank Sr.'s death. Maybe she would have been the huge star if she'd had a better singing voice.

But Dad had to pull away from his mother in order to become his own person. He's told the story several times of standing up at his twenty-first birthday party and declaring that he wasn't going to sing his dad's songs anymore, which made his mother none too happy.

He never told me this directly, but I know he regrets that they weren't getting along when she died. That makes me feel so bad for him. But what makes me most sad is that my grandmother died so young and missed so many happy things: my parents getting married and the huge star my dad became in the music business. She missed seeing her grandchildren grow up. And she missed seeing how every year the legacy of my grandfather Hank Williams continues to grow.

Recently, I was visiting the enormous and absolutely amazing exhibit *Family Tradition: The Williams Family Legacy* at the Country Music Hall of Fame and Museum in Nashville. It's beyond belief to see literally thousands of artifacts, videos, and interactive displays about my own family. But of all the cool things in the exhibit, I found myself staring the longest and hardest at things that belonged to Audrey.

Okay, I'm a girl, and I guess it's easy to understand why I would gawk at her jewelry and clothes. Some of the things are so beautiful—I wanted to steal them out of the glass cases and take them home! But it seemed like the ghost of my grandmother was everywhere. Before leaving the museum, I took a detour into the Brenda Lee exhibit. In a tall glass case in the center of the room, a dress and a gorgeous white mink stole worn by "Little Miss Dynamite" caught my eye. (Window shopping again!)

When I looked closer and read the plaque, it said, "Given to Brenda Lee on the occasion of her high school prom by Audrey Williams." It took my breath away. Here were fifty-foot signs all around the museum and all over town with pictures of my grandfather and my dad, but my eye went right to something that my grandmother once wrapped around Brenda Lee's shoulders.

For the next year or so, Dad endured a series of reconstructive surgeries—nine in all. According to Mom, he was an easy patient who never complained and didn't sit around feeling sorry for himself. He was determined to sing and perform again, so he did everything his doctors told him to do.

He was especially determined to hunt again, and even though at first he had to retrain himself to shoot using his left instead of his right eye, he was out stalking game soon enough. Hunting was always a way to reward himself for milestones in his life—including his recovery.

In fact, after one of his later surgeries, he celebrated afterward with a trip to Idaho to hunt mountain lions. While on that trip, though, the wire that held together the right side of his face broke, and his newly reconstructed cheek and eye rotated upward. He dutifully called his doctors, who gave him the okay to finish the hunt. After he got his lion, he went immediately back to the hospital.

In May 1976, only nine months after he fell off the side of a mountain, Dad returned to the stage. According to him, he kind of snuck out there. For the press, fans, and people in the music business, it wasn't an earthshaking event. But to him, it was huge.

He played almost entirely his own music, and the audience was much younger than his earlier crowds who had come to see the reincarnation of Hank Williams.

The next month, my parents were married at a little church in my mom's hometown of Mer Rouge, followed by a reception at my grandparents' house. It's ironic, but people who grow up in small towns often have huge weddings because they feel like they have to invite the whole town. A town of only a thousand people is small until you think about serving every one of them dinner.

The first guest list that Granny made had 700 names on it! But Dad really didn't want a big wedding, partly because that's not really his style and partly because this was his third marriage. My mother understood how he felt, so they cut the list to 150.

Even though things got a little crazy the week before the wedding, with rumors of celebrities flying in—someone even called my grandparents' house and asked if Dolly Parton was there— most of the guests at the ceremony and reception were family and close friends. There were a few music-business people, including Merle Kilgore and Jerry Rivers, who played in both Dad's and Grandpa's bands. Waylon Jennings and Jessi Colter showed up in a limo that brought them to the wedding directly from a show. Jessi and Waylon were wearing jeans, which evidently raised some eyebrows among some of the "old guard" in the conservative town. "Seat them in the back of the church," one lady sniffed. When my mom got wind of that, she made sure Jessi and Waylon were escorted to the front row.

During the reception, there was some excitement when a low-flying twin-engine plane buzzed the guests. People probably thought it was a crop duster gone off course, but later, everyone found out that it was Bert Jones, the former LSU star quarterback and Mom's ex-boyfriend from college. (Yes, she was Homecoming Queen and dated the quarterback.) I guess Bert, who went on to play for the Baltimore Colts and remains a family friend to this day, wanted to make his presence known. But as my Aunt Jo Lynn told him, "You dated my sister for five years. You had your chance." (Well, what she actually said was, "Shit or get off the pot!")

When I look at their wedding pictures, I think they look so happy. My mom looks gorgeous, although I have to laugh a little when I look at her hair. The night before the wedding, for some reason she decided to give herself an impromptu haircut. She took a pair of scissors and snipped her long, blond hair around her face so she had Farrah Fawcett wings. Wedding pictures are forever, Mom!

After the wedding, Mom and Dad went to Montana for a three-week honeymoon trip. But it wasn't exactly a pampered, four-star resort-type trip. They stayed with my Dad's friends and did a lot of their own cooking.

The next year, they went on a big trip to Africa, which was kind of like a bonus honeymoon. They went with another couple on a safari in Botswana. It's a good thing my mom grew up a country girl and a tomboy because, as amazing as the scenery and the experience was, this was a really rustic trip.

They stayed in tents with dirt floors and slept on army cots. The bathroom was an outhouse, and the shower was a bucket that hung over a tree. They had to walk for miles in 115-degree heat—which at least was dry heat, not humid like Nashville—so she ended up losing a lot of weight. They ate well some nights, but some days they'd just sit in the shade under a tree and pull out fruit and open a can of tuna for lunch.

Even though Mom went hunting with her dad while she was growing up, she wasn't a hard-core hunter. Mostly, she hunted for birds—ducks and wild doves—although she did go wild boar hunting once. Still, she decided to make the trip as a non-hunter. Then, in the middle of the hunt, the guide called an audible: He said, "Miss Becky, come up here. You're going to shoot this buffalo."

She was scared; the herd was only fifteen feet away and there was a buffalo looking right at her. Nonetheless, she took aim, fired her gun, and got that buffalo in one shot. Dad got a buffalo, too, but it took him three shots. Later that day, she shot a zebra. She still has the rug in her house.

Even though that trip is one of her fondest memories, Mom hasn't hunted in years. It's probably not something she would do these days, but back then, that was their lifestyle. You couldn't hang out with my dad and not hunt and fish. Even today, if you want to hang out with him, you better be willing to get up at 5:30 in the morning and traipse through the woods.

Chapter 4

Growing Up

When I was born on February 26, 1979, I set the record for being the longest baby—23 inches—ever born at the hospital in Cullman, Alabama. The first thing my dad said when he saw me was, "She's all arms and legs!"

I haven't checked lately, but as far as I know, the record still stands.

My mom picked the name "Hilary" out of a baby name book, just because she liked it, and gave me my middle name, "June," after her mother. So Mom and Dad took their nearly two-foot-long baby home to their cabin in the tiny Alabama town where they were living, and life changed immediately.

At first, the biggest change was getting up early. For the previous few years, my parents had been keeping musicians' hours—up late, sleep late—and now, they had to get up early every morning. Well, Mom did anyway.

Having a newborn at home was really scary for my mom the first days and weeks because, oddly enough, she had never taken care of a baby before in her entire life. When she was a teenager, she never babysat like most young girls do. In the small Louisiana town where she grew up, a lot of families had housekeepers, most of them older black women who were like part of the family, so there was no need for teenagers to babysit younger siblings or other kids in the neighborhood.

After I was born, my grandmother June came to help, and my great aunt Loretta, my grandmother Audrey's sister, who lived nearby came over, too. My mom didn't even know how to hold me; she was afraid that if she held me too tight she'd smoosh me. Aunt Loretta would say, "Relax, Becky!" She picked me up and cradled my head as she laid me in Mom's arms and showed her what to do.

If Aunt Loretta or my grandmother weren't around, Mom would read baby books and look up answers to her questions. When I got a little colicky or when I wouldn't sleep, Mom figured things out with a little help from Dr. Spock's *Baby and Child Care*.

Mom says for the most part, I was a really good baby. "Easy" is how she puts it. All I did was eat and sleep, and I didn't cry a lot. I don't know if that's true, but I want to believe it. She says, like most babies, I'd wake up really early but I wouldn't cry. I'd just lie in my crib cooing and "singing" until someone came and got me.

When my sister, Holly, was born two years later, it was a different deal. She made a lot of noise and wouldn't sleep. Mom got really worried and asked the doctor and Aunt Loretta why this baby wasn't sleeping. Looking back, this makes complete sense. Holly didn't want to miss anything. Our personalities were in place, right from the start.

As I learned to walk and Holly started to crawl, Dad's career was skyrocketing. He'd been slowly but surely adding to his fan base ever since he hit the road again after recovering from the accident when he fell off the mountain in Montana. He was sticking to his guns, too—making the kind of music he wanted to make. And it was working. By the early 1980s, hits such as "Whiskey Bent and Hellbound" and "All My Rowdy Friends Are Coming Over Tonight" catapulted him to the top of the country outlaw–country rocker heap.

Of course, I was clueless about this at the time. I was much more interested in my blankie than "Born to Boogie."

Mom joined him on the road a few times during the year or two after I was born, and sometimes I would go, too. I have a faint memory of sitting off to the side of the stage, wearing ear plugs, and falling asleep in Mom's lap, right in the middle of the show. But as a rule, it didn't really work to bring me along and Mom didn't like to leave me. So she mostly stayed home. This made for a lot of lonely times for her at home in Alabama. She had help during the week, but on the weekends, with Dad away, she was often at home alone in the country with two little babies.

When Dad was home, he would feed us, sing to us, and even change diapers if Mom asked him to, although she didn't ask him to do things like that very often. She really saw it as her job.

When my dad wasn't traveling, there were many sweet, happy moments. I love closing my eyes and imagining him at home, content and at peace. I picture him scribbling down the words to "Blues Man," the song he wrote for my mom when I was just a few days old. When I was two or three, I remember sitting on his lap and plunking at the strings on his guitar or sitting next to him at the piano. And I remember him smiling a lot.

One thing I don't remember is my mom crying or saying angry things when my parent's marriage began to deteriorate.

I was four years old and Holly was two when my parents separated. The bottom line was that Dad was gone all the time. He toured some three hundred days a year when we were little and continued to do so throughout most of the '80s. And when he was gone, well, as Mom puts it, "He was used to a very different lifestyle."

I know now that she was very hurt when she found out "a different lifestyle" meant more than just a little partying on the road. It meant hard partying with drinking, drugs, and other women. She was devoted to him and had married for life, wanting very much to emulate her parents' fifty-plus-year marriage. She was devastated that her marriage was breaking up. But even though Mom may have been sorely tempted sometimes, she never said a bad word about my father in front of Holly and me. Never.

When my parents separated, Holly and I didn't really notice anything different. Dad was already gone most of the time anyway. The only difference was that now he would be gone all of the time.

My parents actually went back and forth during the next couple of years, almost reconciling several times. Then, one day, after yet another attempt to get back together, Dad left and stayed gone for several months. Mom knew she had to make the decision to end their unhealthy relationship. So she filed for divorce.

I don't think Dad even talked to her about it when she filed. And there was no big, final, knock-down, drag-out fight. One day she just got divorce papers back in the mail and that was it.

One night when Holly, Mom, and I were sitting at the dinner table, Mom decided it was time to tell us about the divorce. She tried to be very nonchalant about it, saying, "Girls, your dad and I are going to be getting a divorce. Eat your broccoli, please."

Holly, who was five years old, didn't bat an eye: "But I don't like broccoli . . . "

But I was a wise seven-year-old and I knew that divorce was bad. Even though our lives would essentially be no different, the word bothered me and I burst out crying. I couldn't escape the nagging feeling that the divorce was somehow my fault. I know a lot of kids feel this way, and when you get older, you work on convincing yourself that it isn't true. But when you're five and six and seven years old, the thoughts creep into your head: "Did I do something? Maybe he doesn't like me? Maybe he has another secret family somewhere?" Crazy things.

Although she didn't show it, my mom was really hurting inside. The thing is that I truly believe my parents loved each other. Their lives and expectations were just too different.

It broke Mom's heart to think that we would never have what she had—a full-time, hands-on dad. Mom had her daddy around her all her life. She and my grandfather were always riding horses together or riding around in his pick-up truck when Mom was young, and her dad was there every night to eat dinner with her and tell her he loved her.

Mom felt like she had failed us, but she always kept up an incredibly strong, positive front. For the most part, we didn't feel that bad, although sometimes we'd see other kids with their dads around and we'd get a little melancholy. One time, Holly was at the playground and told Mom she wished she had a daddy to swing her, like her friend did. But mostly, this was our life—and we were used to it.

People are surprised when I tell them that my parents' divorce wasn't ugly: no huge fights, no yelling, no battle over money or custody of the kids. My dad took responsibility for their split and they settled out of court.

It helped that he has always taken care of us financially, although we weren't rich by any means. Mom, Holly, and I lived frugally. I remember being out to dinner when we were kids and ordering water instead of soda to keep the bill down. When we were teenagers, some of our friends whose dads were doctors or lawyers would take their parents' credit cards and spend $1,000 at the mall. Holly and I would save up our money for a shirt at the Gap, or we shopped at Target. Things were normal. We were typical middle-class kids.

After the divorce, we moved from Alabama to Nashville, where Mom lived before she got married and where she knew some people. Even though we were in Nashville, where many music business people live, most of our friends were from school or church. The exception was Waylon Jennings and his wife, Jessi Colter, who were two of Mom and Dad's closest friends. One of the best times Mom ever had was attending a party at Waylon and Jessi's house. It was a sobriety party for Johnny Cash. Obviously, no one drank alcohol at the party, and for some reason, there was a '50s theme. Mom even wore a poodle skirt! Both Mom and Dad remained close to Jessi and Waylon after my parents split up.

Holly, Mom, and I used to visit the Jennings house all the time and swim in their pool. We'd drive up to their driveway, where they had a security gate with a guard sitting in a shack with a TV and a callbox. I remember thinking that the shack was the security guy's house (I guess that's what a little kid would think) and wondered why it was so small.

Out front, there were always a couple of tour buses and a bunch of cars parked in the driveway; they had several of the same model Mercedes, all in different colors. The house itself was awesome, but being so young, Holly and I only really paid attention to the kid-specific, fun stuff. We used to head straight for the zip line they had in their backyard and take turns flying down it with their son, Shooter, who is my age. Then we'd go inside to one of the bathrooms and watch the water spray up when we pushed the handle on the porcelain fixture next to the toilet. "Girls, that's a bidet," Jessi told me and Holly. We stared at her blankly. "It cleans you off after you've done your business." After she told us that, we left it alone.

I remember that Shooter had so many toys and stuffed animals that it looked like Toys "R" Us in his room. (Shooter's real name is Waylon Albright Jennings, Jr., but his parents nicknamed him "Shooter" the day he was born. Shooter says his mom had a friend whose son was named Shooter and they thought it was cool, but according to his dad, they called him Shooter because he peed on the baby nurse when she was changing his diaper. Maybe it was a combination of both.) It's funny to imagine Shooter with stuffed animals or as a baby, sitting in his crib, riding along on the tour bus with his parents, the outlaws!

Shooter also had three computers—those huge ones that take up your whole desk. This was back when no one had PCs, so three computers all lined up in a row looked wild to us, like *Star Trek* or something. And his birthday parties were also incredible, with bouncy houses and games all set up in the backyard. It looked like we were going to the circus or a big carnival.

When we were growing up, I thought Shooter was kind of nerdy, but now I know he was just quiet and a little bit shy. These days, he's Mr. Rock-and-Roller, out touring with Alice in Chains. He's had a couple of different bands that play country and rock and Southern rock; it's kind of hard to categorize his music. And why do people always want to do that, anyway?

When we were both just out of high school, Shooter was recording some of his rock material in a studio he'd set up in his parents' pool house. The recording "booth" was actually the pool house closet. One day, he asked me to come over and sing backup on a demo of one of his rock songs. I said, "Sure. I'm not a screamer, but I'll give it a shot!"

I don't even remember what song it was; I don't think he ever released it. But it sounded good. There were some first-rate acoustics in that closet!

When we were little kids, neither Shooter nor Holly and I ever realized that each other's dads were somebody special. Back then, Shooter thought our dad was just this regular old guy and we thought Shooter's dad was just a really nice man who teased my mom about her Louisiana accent and who came outside in his pajamas, sat in the big rocking chair, and watched us swim. To us, Waylon's wife was an incredibly sweet lady and my mom's friend who made iced tea by brewing it out in the sun and then served it to us with fresh sprigs of mint. But as we got a little older, we realized that Waylon was a huge star. That's him and Jessi—and with Willie Nelson and Tompall Glaser—on the cover of *Wanted! The Outlaws!* I remember hearing "I'm Not Lisa," that big hit song from the '70s on the radio one day. We were driving along and my mom said, "That's Jessi . . ."

I said, "Jessi's singing?"

"Yes!" Mom said. "And she wrote it, too!"

I think I was a teenager when I found out that Waylon played with Buddy Holly back in the late '50s and was the one who gave up his seat on the plane to the Big Bopper the night of the fatal plane crash. In fact, I learned about it when Waylon and Dad were featured on a CMT show about country stars that cheated death. Anyway, eventually we were clued in, but our two families treated each other normally. The stardom—and certainly the drugs and outrageousness—were separate from our times together.

Mom really leaned on Jessi when we first moved to Nashville. When she felt overwhelmed or frustrated or when the sadness began to overtake her, she would go over to Jessi's house and sit on the floor of her bedroom and just cry and cry while Jessi hugged her and prayed for her. Jessi lives in Phoenix now, but she and Mom still call each other every month or so, and they swear they'll get together soon.

And of course everybody misses Waylon, who died in 2002. Dad loved him so much. They first met in the 1960s when Waylon was one of the many acts touring with my grandmother Audrey's Caravan of Stars. At age fourteen, Dad was the headliner then, but later, in the late '70s, Dad opened for Waylon. They used to kid each other, "You carried me, now I'll carry you, then later, you can carry me again . . ."

I love the story Dad tells about ditching his mother and sneaking over to Waylon's bus during the Caravan of Stars. Dad was too young to drive, but one day he convinced Waylon's bus driver to let him take the bus for a spin. He then proceeded to drive the bus right off the road and knocked all the hubcaps off the tires!

Waylon and Dad collaborated musically many times. Waylon produced Dad's 1977 album, *The New South*, the first album he recorded after his mountain fall, and it was a great experience. Waylon listened to Dad's ideas and Dad trusted Waylon, so they really meshed.

Obviously, Waylon was a major Hank Williams, Sr., fan, which he gave away in songs such as "Are You Sure Hank Done It This Way" and "The Conversation," and once, Dad gave him a pair of his daddy's cowboy boots. As Dad tells it, Waylon pulled them on right away and they fit him perfectly.

A year or two after Waylon died, I met Dad where he was staying at the Hermitage Hotel in downtown Nashville. I was waiting for him out front when he pulled up in a yellow, late-1970s two-door Lincoln he had just bought. (Dad just loves those old cars.) "Check this out," he said, as he popped a tape into the vintage eight-track player. Then we took off and rode around all afternoon playing and singing along to nothing but Waylon Jennings songs. Dad looked really, really happy.

My parents' split and our move to Nashville were major childhood milestones, but possibly my most life-changing event, until the accident anyway, happened when I was eight years old and I found out that I had diabetes.

For a couple of months, I had been losing weight and I was thirsty all the time. Mom would give me Gatorade, which is full of glucose and one of the worst things for a child with diabetes to drink. But she didn't know that at the time. There was no diabetes in her family and she really didn't know much about it. I mean, kids get thirsty. She never suspected that something was seriously wrong.

I really wasn't a sickly or a whiny kid, but all of the sudden, I felt sick all the time. I was always exhausted, and every morning

I'd tell Mom that I just couldn't get out of bed. She'd feel my fore-head and see that I didn't have a fever and tell me to get up. She thought I was just being lazy and didn't want to go to school.

"You'll be fine," she said.

One morning I insisted, "Mother, I can't go to school! I'm too weak!" I never pushed like that or yelled at Mom. Well, at least I didn't when I was eight.

So I stayed home, and Mom wondered what in the world had gotten into me. Then my Aunt Jo Lynn came over and convinced her that I didn't look well at all. "Look at her, Becky!" Jo Lynn said. "That child's lost twenty pounds!"

Because Aunt Jo Lynn didn't see me every day like Mom did, Jo Lynn could tell that I looked different and things weren't right. She'd also recently dreamed that I was in the hospital, which spooked Mom because Jo Lynn was known to have really good intuition.

Aunt Jo Lynn and I always had a special connection. For some reason, she always doted on me. When I was little, I'd jump into her arms, wrap my legs around her waist, and say, "Uncle Jo Lynn!" (I also called her then-husband, Joe Stampley, "Uncle Joe Lynn," which they all thought was hilarious.) Maybe I was so attached to her because, truth be told, I was a little afraid of Uncle Joe when I was little. I wasn't used to men being around, and he used to wear this velour track suit with the jacket zipped halfway down with his chest hairs sticking out. That's scary, right?

I also loved the way Aunt Jo Lynn handled Dad so well. One night many years ago, Dad called Jo Lynn at 4:00 in the morning and asked if she'd go get him some Krystal burgers. He was in Nashville working on a record and staying at Spence Manor on Music Row, and at the time, Jo Lynn lived in Antioch, which was a good thirty minutes away. Plus, it was 4:00 in the morning. "Why don't you call a cab, Hank?" she said.

Well, he did call a cab, but he didn't get in the cab. He asked the driver to go get the burgers and bring them back to him. And the guy did it!

Another time, Jo Lynn and her then-husband and Mom and Dad were out to dinner when Dad got up to go to the restroom. A long time passed and he wasn't coming out. Then, someone went to check on him, and evidently, he'd gone out the bathroom window. Outside, someone from the restaurant saw him and asked him what was wrong. He said, "The food was no good." Then he hopped in a cab and left. Well, the waiter came to the table and said, "Mr. Williams didn't care for the food so the check is on us."

Jo Lynn said, "No sir, the food is just fine. The check is on Mr. Williams. Becky, give the man his credit card."

Anyway, as she would do many times over the years, Aunt Jo Lynn spoke up for me when I was eight years old and not feeling well, so we went to the doctor. After running some tests, the doctor came in the room. "Hilary has juvenile diabetes," he said.

My blood sugar was reading around 800—normal ranges from 80 to 120. So they put me in the hospital right away. Because I was only eight years old, I didn't realize how serious this was. I had juvenile diabetes, or type 1 diabetes, which is the type of the disease generally diagnosed in children, teenagers, or young adults. Nobody knows for sure what causes it, but it's most likely a combination of genetics and environmental factors, like stress or trauma. It's weird, though: Nobody who we know of in my family has diabetes. Some people speculate that my grandfather Hank Williams may have had it and not known it, but other than that, it isn't prevalent on either side. So no one knows why I got it, but I had it nonetheless.

Basically, type 1 diabetes is a disorder of the body's immune system, which, when it's working properly, fights off viruses and other unhealthy things. But the immune system of a person with diabetes attacks and destroys certain cells in the pancreas, making it impossible to produce insulin. With no insulin, glucose, a form of sugar, stays in the blood instead of moving throughout the body to provide energy. So people with type 1 diabetes need to take insulin for energy and to stay alive.

As I climbed into my hospital bed, I wasn't thinking about the fact that I would be dealing with this every day for the rest of my life. Mostly, I just remember feeling kind of grouchy. The kids in my class sent me cards and notes, which cheered me up some. And a nurse took me down to look at the newborn babies, which definitely lifted my spirits. They even let me hold a tiny, premature baby who weighed only three pounds and fit in the palm of my hand. I couldn't believe they let me do that. It was so cool.

Then I started feeling grouchy again. Someone at the hospital—I don't remember who—asked me if I'd like to be in the newspaper ("Hank Jr.'s Daughter Diagnosed with Diabetes"). I definitely wanted no part of that. Then I overheard someone say something about, "no candy," and I didn't like that either.

The truth was that I really wasn't much of a candy-eater anyway. Aunt Jo Lynn would bring us Rolos and M&M's, and I'd leave them in my room untouched for weeks. In fact, my favorite "treat" was V-8 juice. I used to drink a ton of it. Looking back, I think it was just the new rules that I didn't like. Then, a nurse came in and pricked my finger to test my blood sugar. That I definitely didn't like! As she wrapped a Band-Aid around my finger, the nurse explained that it can be dangerous—even life-threatening—for a person with diabetes to let her blood sugar get too high or too low. So I—or Mom, until I learned to do it myself—would have to test my blood sugar four times a day. Every day. From then on.

I would also need to learn how to give myself daily insulin shots. So the nurses brought in some oranges and needles and told me to practice with them. What? Stick this orange with a needle? Now stick myself? I wanted to crawl under the covers and forget the whole thing. But I didn't have a choice. Bring on the oranges!

After practicing on the fruit for a day or two, Mom bravely let me stick her with a needle before I tried it on myself. I couldn't believe it when Aunt Jo Lynn, who despises needles, let me stick her, too. Then, Dad came to the hospital and Aunt Jo Lynn, said, "Okay, Hank. It's your turn."

Without missing a beat, my Dad turned his back and dropped his pants. "Okay, I'm ready!"

The look on the nurse's face was priceless.

I burst out laughing, but Aunt Jo Lynn just shook her head. "Next time," she said, "Your arm will do just fine."

After three days, I was released from the hospital. When I first got home, I felt really down. I remember lying in bed that night and worrying about this diabetes thing: All these shots. Am I going to be sick all the time?

Then I started feeling sad about my dad being gone. I was crying softly, trying not to let Holly or Mom hear me, when all of a sudden, this incredible feeling of peace washed over me. I looked up and there was a white light, kind of a glow in my room. I saw this giant, life-sized figure with his hand stretched out. It was Jesus—right there in my room. He picked me up like a baby and held me for a minute. I guess he was letting me know everything was going to be alright. Then he backed out and went away. I went right to sleep, and when I woke up, it was as if my worries had floated away. I know it sounds crazy, but it was amazing and it happened and I don't have the words for how much it comforted me.

The next day, diabetes became just a regular part of my life. Mom's and Holly's lives, too. It was hard for Holly, who was only six when I first got diagnosed. What six-year-old is cool with not having candy in the house? Though sometimes, Aunt Jo Lynn felt bad for her and would sneak her some.

Going back to school that first week was kind of tough. The boys in my class teased me relentlessly. They'd come up behind me and yell, "Hilary has cooties!"—as if diabetes is some contagious airborne disease or something you get from not washing your hands.

In the beginning, Mom was nervous giving me shots, which is understandable. She was afraid she would hit a blood vessel or a vein and hurt me. But she got better and better at it. I did, too. Soon, I was able to give myself a shot without even looking. Usually, I'd lift up my shirt and stick myself in the stomach; it's easier than trying to reach around and give myself a shot in the arm using only one hand. At school, I'd almost always go into the bathroom and slip into a stall to check my blood sugar or give myself shots with the prefilled needle I'd carry around in its handy little case. These days, I just do it wherever, like in the car or sometimes even at the table in the restaurant. If I look down and do it fast, no one even notices.

But no matter how good you are about checking your levels and taking insulin shots, inevitably, every person with diabetes experiences an unexpected drop in blood sugar. Sometimes people lose consciousness or sometimes they even go into a diabetic coma. Thankfully, that's never happened to me. But I have to be prepared.

Mom always carried glucose tablets or little pieces of candy in her purse, just in case of an emergency. And one time, while we were at church—I think I was twelve years old—all of the sudden I felt faint and almost passed out on the floor. I needed sugar really badly. That was the only time I remember Mom not having glucose tablets with her, so we rushed out of church and went to the Taco Bell drive-thru to get a Coke.

Another time, Mom came in and found me lying on the kitchen floor. I wasn't passed out—just dizzy. She gave me some juice, and just like that, I was up and running around, having forgotten the whole thing.

Probably the biggest scare I can remember was when a group of us from my high school went on a two-week trip to a Christian camp in Northern California. I was expecting Kumbaya and marshmallows by the campfire, but instead I got *Survivor: Eureka, California.*

One day, we hiked way out in the wilderness, where we were supposed to spend twenty-four hours with God. That is, sleep out all night under the stars—alone. But I had trouble during the hike because we were supposed to eat very little—kind of a pseudo-fast—so I had to borrow food from other kids to keep my blood sugar from dropping. However, we lucked out when it started to hail and the counselors let us sleep together in a big tent. But it was cold and my insulin froze solid. It was a miracle that the tube didn't break; if it had, I don't know what we would have done. There were no cell phones back then, and the nearest hospital was hours away. Anyway, it defrosted enough to use the next morning.

Then, the next night, we were sent out to complete our twenty-four hours with God. As I walked off by myself, I was really scared. All I could think about was mountain lions and bears, so when I heard a couple of girls nearby I whispered loudly, "Over here!" and we all huddled next to each other in our sleeping bags for the entire night. I didn't think God would mind.

Being a kid with diabetes isn't as bad as being a teenager with diabetes. No teenager wants to be different than everybody else, so sometimes I'd be less than consistent about checking my levels. Then, if I got tired or really thirsty, or if I got a headache, I'd try to keep it to myself. If I had to miss gym class, I'd try not to make a big deal of it. If there was cake at a birthday party, I'd just have a little bit and then take my insulin right away.

I've always been pretty good about my diet, but I remember when I was first diagnosed, I went to see a nutritionist who was a little extreme. He showed me the food pyramid, and that made sense, but then he wanted me to drink cod liver oil and eat nothing but fish. This guy also wanted me to drink four glasses of milk a day, which I did for a while. But I kept getting ear and sinus infections, so I went to an allergist who diagnosed me with a serious milk allergy. So no more milk for me.

These days, people are more educated about carbs and the glycemic index—all the things people with diabetes have known about for years. Basically, people with diabetes benefit from eating the way any healthy person would. Low (but not *no*) carbohydrates, whole grains, lean protein, and, of course, easy on the sugar. It used to be that I had to time my meals precisely and take short-acting insulin right before I ate. Now, however, it's easier because I take long-acting insulin that lasts twenty-four hours. It manages my blood sugar so much better, and I don't have to think about food constantly.

When I was a teenager, I could never get my blood sugar under 200, but I'm proud to say that over the last few years, my hemoglobin A1C tests, the diagnostics that provide an average of one's blood sugar over a six-to-twelve-week period, have been in the "six" range, which is good. My doctor says the readings are similar to that of a person without diabetes.

Of course I'm talking about the years before and after the wreck. During the months I was in the hospital, well, that was a different story.

Chapter 5

Up and Down

The next couple of weeks in Memphis felt like a roller-coaster ride—the old, wooden, scary kind of roller-coaster ride, where the tracks creak as the car inches around rickety corners. There's a little dip, and then you ride along smoothly before you take the really big plunge. You fall and fall and scream as your stomach drops. You try to put your hands in the air, but mostly, you hold on tight. Then you hit bottom and exhale as you slowly bump your way back up to the top.

Several doctors and nurses confided to me later that they were stunned that I had survived the accident at all, let alone the nine major and five minor surgeries I had during my time at the Med. They also told me they were surprised I was able to keep all my limbs.

I am so grateful to the amazing people who saved my life and took care of me in the hospital. I wish I could remember more particulars of each procedure. In a way, it's kind of spooky to lose that many days of my life.

The truth is, though, that all the surgeries blend together in my mind. It's almost impossible to separate one from the other. Usually, a nurse would come in and mark part of my body with a marker, so there would be no confusion about which leg or hip or side of this or that bone they would cut into later. Then someone would move me onto a cold, hard, metal X-ray table. (I understand why they can't be padded, but do they have to be cold?)

I'd try not to cry out as my broken body was shifted onto a stretcher and wheeled into an operating room where the anesthesiologist would read a list of risks—suffocation, allergic reaction, organ failure, stroke, death—before he inserted an IV into my arm and put a breathing mask on my face. I remember the weird, kind of sour smell and being told to take deep breaths as other people wearing masks and shower caps came into view under the bright white lights. Then I'd wake up later. Hours later? Days later? I'm not sure. I'd be in another room. It was always hard to wake up. I felt heavy and groggy, and sometimes I couldn't move or speak, but I could hear and I could feel pain creeping over me like thick morning fog.

Next, someone would give me painkillers. Sometimes it was morphine, which at first felt like fire coursing through my veins. It dulled the pain but made me itch violently. You never hear about that in movies, where wounded soldiers are given morphine on the battlefield or dying patients push the button to administer their own morphine drip. None of them complain about itching or burning. They just want more.

I wanted the pain to stop, but the painkillers caused allergic reactions (so I'd always have to take Benadryl), and worse, they made me sick, sometimes violently so. I'd vomit—and that hurt—and then I'd wonder if the pain medicine had gone from my body? Did I need more? Or less? Back on the roller coaster.

One thing I had to get used to in Memphis was people staring at me. Not my family or visitors so much as doctors, nurses, and interns. They came in my room a lot, and when they did, they spent a lot of time looking at me.

The Med is a major teaching hospital, so the staff doctors often brought medical students to my bedside—sometimes ten, twelve, or more at a time—to show them my injuries and demonstrate what to do or, sometimes, what *not* to do. Some of the residents were young, not much older than me, and most of them were male and many of them were disarmingly good looking.

I remember one day when a group of them left the room after looking at an open fracture, the exposed bone near my ankle, where I would eventually get a skin flap to cover it. "Hilary!" Mom said, as they walked out the door with their clipboards under their arms. "Those are some of the cutest young men!"

As much as I might have wanted to meet a cute young doctor, it wasn't exactly my idea of a great first date. I felt ghoulish, like a circus freak or a wax museum statue. The students must have known I was uncomfortable having my body displayed like that. They were all as respectful and as considerate as they could be in a situation like that. One resident, Billy Graves, who went on to practice as an oral maxillofacial surgeon in Amarillo, Texas, was especially sweet to me. One day he came in my room with a big stack of e-mails in his hand; he'd surprised me by going to my MySpace page and printing out all the messages I got from friends and friends of friends. That was so cool—so above and beyond what he had to do as a resident.

Then, while he was keeping me company, I'd ask him about what a maxillofacial surgeon does. My fault for asking. Basically, that type of surgeon puts people's faces back together. He showed me some pretty gnarly pictures. Then, when we were talking one time—again, my fault for asking questions—he told me, "If you're trying to commit suicide, you should never shoot yourself in the mouth. It won't kill you. It just blows your face off." Good to know.

I met so many great people at the Med, such as the sweet physical therapist who came in and smiled and encouraged me and whenever I did the smallest thing. He'd say, "You're a star! You're a star!" Actually, he had an Asian accent (I think he was originally from China), and it sounded more like, "You a stah! You a stah!" It cracked me up every time. I just loved him.

It seemed that every day someone would surprise me with yet another random act of kindness. We'd hear things about people talking about us on shows; for instance, on *Nashville Star*, Wynonna Judd said, "Everyone please pray for the Williams sisters." Holly and I got dozens of cards and gifts from friends and from Dad's fans. A couple of our favorites were these adorable Vermont teddy bears, one dressed in a hospital gown, one dressed in a ballerina outfit. We still have those! We got so many flowers, which killed me because I couldn't have them in my room, though Mom took pictures to show me all of them. But it was great; we just shared them with other patients and the nurses. It was as if a garden had sprung up at the Med.

There were plenty of bold-faced names on some of the gift cards, too. Sean Hannity, a friend of Dad's, sent a beautiful bouquet, and Tim McGraw and Faith Hill, also friends of Dad's, sent a huge spray to the hospital and, later, food to our house. Keith Urban also sent food to the house, and that first week we were in the hospital, he called Holly's management company every day to find out how we were doing. We got presents from other people in the music industry, too, including Kix Brooks and Ronnie Dunn as well as Del Bryant, President of BMI, who sent a big basket of cheeses and cookies. Mom still has the basket in her kitchen. The producer Tony Brown and his then-wife, Anastasia, sent a CD player, CDs of soothing music, and gifts from a day spa.

And the nurses! As if they weren't already doing enough, they also baked cakes for my family and brought me gifts, including a beautiful flannel blanket. Stephanie's eight-year-old boy drew me a picture, and I put it up in my room. Angel, one of the sweetest nurses ever, used to tell me, "Pringles and sweet tea always make me feel better." Then, later, a can of Pringles would show up on my tray.

The kindness extended beyond the nurse's station, too. Once, when I was recovering in post-op, a nun sat down beside me and asked if she could pray for me. I nodded yes, of course.

I was really happy when, later, Dad sent a big fruit basket to every nurse in the ER I felt that that was the least we could do.

Even as there are many good memories I have from Memphis, there also are some—one having nothing to do with the hospital— that I wish I could erase entirely. I'm talking about the bogus (in my opinion) accusation made against my dad by a cocktail wait-ress who worked in the bar at the Peabody Hotel. Obviously, be-cause it was just three days after the wreck, I wasn't there the night in question. But after comparing the news report and hear-ing from people who were there, including Dad, I think the inci-dent was blown out of proportion.

The waitress said Dad harassed her and physically assaulted her. I think that words were exchanged, and then he tried to smooth it over and went to hug her—not put her in a chokehold as she claimed.

I think someone wanted money. It burns me up that he had to call a press conference in front of the hospital while Holly and I were upstairs in the ICU in order to deal with that and another stupid rumor, which spread when someone called a radio talk show and said they overheard Hank Jr. saying he only wanted white people to work on his daughters.

There are other things I try to forget. Like the morning that first week in Memphis that I woke up in handcuffs—real metal handcuffs. Like the kind that the police use when they are re-straining criminals.

I was kind of bleary and disoriented after surgery, so it took me a minute, but when the daze lifted, I realized that both of my hands were handcuffed to the bedrails along each side of the bed. "Oh my gosh," I thought. "What did I do? Am I in the loony bin?"

When the nurse walked in, I opened my eyes and, because I didn't have much of a voice, whispered, "Why am I handcuffed to the bed?"

"You keep pulling out the tubes," she said, readjusting the line that fed from my nose and throat to the ventilator. The tubes were back in my mouth so I couldn't explain to her that I was coughing so hard that they kept coming out. I started drifting back off to sleep, so I made a mental note to tell her about the coughing later. Soon after, when the handcuffs were gone, a different nurse was in the room when I started coughing loud and hard. "Are you a singer, sweetie?" she asked.

I nodded yes.

"Well, that's not a surprise," she said. "I thought you might be. You have such strong lungs!"

Another memory I'd like to erase involved a particularly grueling physical therapy session, one of the first I had. It was just a few days after a surgery to repair my shattered femur, and the therapist came in to help me move from my bed to a chair.

Dr. Croce is a big believer in getting his patients up and moving. As he puts it, you can't fix the fractures if the lungs are no good. Because of all my broken bones, I had to be almost completely immobilized for the first two weeks in the hospital, and that was a concern for the docs at the Med. So whenever possible, they'd try to get me to get up. Not to just sit up in bed, but to get out of bed. So the therapist started to talk me through the process. "Okay, Hilary, use your arms to push up. Now move your legs to the side . . ."

I tried really hard to do what he was asking me—in fact, I was doing it—but the metal was shifting in my body and every time

I moved, something sharp jammed into my pelvis. The pain was excruciating! I was hyperventilating, it hurt so badly, and I kept stopping to catch my breath. The therapist was really pushing, "C'mon Hilary, you've got to try!"

I understand this was the guy's job and his heart was in the right place, but it really ticked me off because I was trying! I knew he had patients who didn't try or would only do the minimum. How could I convince him that I wasn't a whiner?

I really, really wanted to do what he was asking but I physically could not do it. Every part of my femur, the thigh bone, had been broken, as well as my hips and tailbone. Did he not know this?

The tears were welling up in my eyes, but I was so mad, I didn't cry. I tried again but the piercing pain stabbed at me again and I started gasping. I thought I was going to black out. In fact, I think I did black out a little bit. When Mom saw that—my sweet, polite, little mom—yelled at the guy, "That's enough! I'm sorry, but that's enough!" Session over.

One day not long after that, Dr. Croce and I were talking about my progress. I asked him whether I would always be in so much pain.

"Pain is a sign of life, Hilary," he answered.

Then he stopped and looked right at me. I think he may have regretted saying that, so he tried to explain. "Those probably aren't very comforting words," he said.

At first, they weren't. I was kind of mad at him for saying them. But the more I thought about it, which was every time I hurt, the more sense it made: No pain, no gain!

I still remember all the pain during those first few weeks, but I think that most human beings have this great capacity to forget, or at least let really bad memories fade—not disappear, but fade.

The pain is still there. I have pain every day and probably will for the rest of my life. But I try not to dwell on it, and through-out my rehab and to this day, I tried to think of pain, at times, like a good sign. As Dr. Croce pointed out, it's just part of being alive.

A lot of people came to see me in the hospital, especially during the first week or so. After Aunt Jo Lynn left, Aunt Donna came for a few days and was a huge help, taking Holly to her doctor's appointments at Campbell Clinic. My family even had a clown come in one day. Basically, he (I think it was a "he") came in, said, "Hi Hilary!" then left. It was really sweet, even if it was a little strange.

The whole time Dad was with me at the hospital, it seemed as if he never left my room. Every time I woke up, he was sitting there beside my bed, usually holding my hand or holding his head in his hands. Holly said he wouldn't even leave when everyone went downstairs to go to lunch. Sometimes, I'd wake up and write him a note—something simple like "Hi" or "I love you" or, once, I wrote "Mr. Weatherman," a song of his I loved, so he sang it to me softly.

It was really dark in my room, especially at first, and there was a curtain and I was sleeping a lot, so besides Mom and Dad, sometimes I didn't even really know who was there. It was so comforting, though, when every time I woke up, Mom would say, "Guess who's here?" or "You won't believe who called this morning."

I was so glad when my cousin Sarah Beth, who is more like a sister than a cousin, came up from Louisiana after my grandfather's funeral and stayed for a few days. Sarah Beth cracked me up when she told me that I'd ruined *Grey's Anatomy* for her. After the accident, she couldn't watch it anymore. I couldn't either, and that used to be my favorite show!

My sister Katie and brother Sam came to visit, too. Even though Sam and Katie are technically my half-brother and -sister, Dad's kids with his wife Mary Jane, I always call them my brother and sister. That's how I feel about them. I was at the hospital the day Katie was born. I got to see her and hold her that day, her very first day on earth. She was so funny. I thought she looked like a conehead. Holly and I were so excited to have a little sister. It was like having a little doll to play with.

We loved taking care of her and our little brother, Sam, when he came along a few years later. Sam is a brilliant kid. When he was five years old, Dad would walk in and catch him reading the newspaper. When he was in the seventh grade, he took the ACT test (college entrance exam) and scored a 24 (the average for high school seniors is 20).

When Sam and Katie were babies, we changed their diapers and fed them and bathed them. We even took baths with them when they were really tiny. Dad has a huge Jacuzzi tub, so we'd put them in there with those floating intertubes. Then, while they were floating and splashing around, Holly and I would hop in the tub with them. It was hilarious.

I used to bathe Sam a lot. He didn't like people to wash his hair, and for a while, he would only let me do it. "You don't let water get in my eyes and ears," he told me.

Holly and I feel like, in some ways, Sam and Katie are our kids. We've taken care of them a lot at different times in their lives, especially when their mom was away receiving treatment for drug and alcohol abuse. We let them stay with us. We take them shopping for school clothes. We answer their calls any time of the day. I couldn't love them any more than I do, even if they were my full brother and sister.

So when they came to the hospital in Memphis, I spent some time with Katie, although she could not stop sobbing, which broke my heart. I didn't get to see Sam because he was only eight years old at the time and wasn't allowed to come into the ICU. He did get in to see Holly, though, which afterward everyone thought was probably a mistake. Mom said when he saw how battered she looked, huge tears started running down his face. It kills me to think of that.

After two days, Holly was released from the hospital and moved into the hotel room with my mom. Although she still had to see doctors as an outpatient the next couple of days, and it was hard for her to get dressed and shower because of the cast on her arm (Sarah Beth helped with that), she immediately shifted out of patient mode and became the leader in my troupe of visitors.

Holly is a really energetic person, and even though she was fresh out of a hospital bed and still had a cast on her arm, as she put it, her legs worked fine so she was constantly coming in and out of my room, bringing in a DVD player or extra pillows. She kept running back and forth nonstop with Detective Dan, taking orders and bringing back barbecue so everyone could take a break from eating in the hospital cafeteria.

She must have been a sight—her face was all cut up, her head was huge, and she had no whites in her eyes. Plus, she was wearing loose hospital scrubs, which were easier to take on and off over her cast. She really stood out, so it wasn't really a surprise when she and Aunt Jo Lynn went to the drugstore and the clerk recognized her: "You're that girl who was in the accident!" the clerk shouted.

Holly turned around, went directly to the rotating sunglasses display, and grabbed a pair of the biggest sunglasses she could find. She quickly paid for them, put them on, and sprinted outside, where Detective Dan had the motor running.

Of all my visitors, one of the real highlights was when Bishop Marvin E. Donaldson, a reverend from Kansas City, came to the hospital to visit and pray with us a day or two after the wreck.

Dad got to know the bishop through his dear friend Derrick Thomas, the Kansas City Chiefs star linebacker who died following a tragic car accident in 2000. Dad wrote the song "Cross on the Highway" from his *Almeria Club* record about Thomas and his friend Mike Telles, who also died in the wreck. He recorded the song at the Greater Pentecostal Temple in Kansas City, Bishop Donaldson's church and the site where Derrick Thomas's memorial service was held.

Dad laughs when he tells people that Bishop Donaldson is the only minister he knows who carries a .38 on a shoulder holster. I guess his church back in Kansas City is in a pretty rough neighborhood. All in all, he's a good man to have around.

After two weeks or so, the flurry of visitors slowed down. Holly went home to Nashville, although she drove back to Memphis several more times while I was there. Dad went home, too. He had to: Katie and Sam needed him there.

I understood that people had to leave and go back to their everyday lives. My surgeries—the big, critical ones anyway—were mostly over. My days had turned from a critical adrenaline rush to wait-and-see. Nonetheless, it was hard to watch people leave. It was kind of like the week or two after a funeral. The really sad part is over but so is all the activity, including the celebrations and all the food and the company coming and going. The reality of the loss sets in later.

So my days in Memphis got longer, and even though I didn't really have a chance to get bored, thanks to lots of *Little Rascals* DVDs, I still couldn't push away the creeping feeling that as everybody went back to their lives, this was my new life: Waiting for the doctor to come in. Talking about the next surgery. Charting the next small step in my recovery.

I tried not to think too far into the future. I knew that healing wasn't going to be easy, and even though I realized that I'd never be the same physically, somehow I knew that everything would be okay. I didn't conjure up particulars. Maybe I had the right "one day at a time" attitude. Or, more likely, I was just clueless.

I didn't hear the doctors say that they doubted I would make it through the first night or subsequent nights, or that at one point, they doubted they'd be able to save my leg. I never heard them say I wouldn't walk again. I didn't hear them say she's probably going to need a hip replacement, and I didn't know that hip replacements usually only last fifteen years.

I didn't truly understand all the risks I incurred during every surgery because of my diabetes and the extreme shock I'd been through and the number of transfusions I had been given. Because I knew so little, I was able to live in denial. Or, as I like to think, I could focus on the positive.

When I'd start to get sad or frustrated—such as the times I'd be slowly coming out of anesthesia and I could see and hear people all around me but couldn't talk or use my hands or even control my fingers to communicate—I'd just take a break and picture something peaceful in my mind's eye. I'd like to claim that my visualizations were amazingly creative and profound, but mostly I just pictured predictable things such as a white, sandy beach and sitting there with a cold Corona in my hand. That usually got me through until I could move or speak again.

A while back I watched a movie called *The Diving Bell and the Butterfly*, based on the memoir by an *Elle* editor, Jean-Dominique Bauby, who had a stroke. The only part of his body that would work was his left eye. He communicated by blinking; each blink stood for a letter: One blink meant the letter "A," two for the letter "B," three for the letter "C," and so forth.

The movie was wild. It was filmed as if the audience is in his body looking out. Anyway, I thought to myself that if he could communicate—after all, this man blinked an entire book!—then I could, too. I could write on the board when I couldn't speak, and I felt lucky that, as frustrating as it was not to be able to move or talk when I wanted to, if I just waited—imaginary Corona in hand—my time would come.

Positive visualization helped me a great deal in the hospital and would help me for years to come. But I was also comforted by thinking about miracles. So whenever I started to feel stressed or scared, I'd make a mental list of all the things that conspired to save Holly and me the day of the wreck. For instance, it had rained the day before the accident, so the ground was muddy, which cushioned the impact of the crash. We were close to Memphis, which has one of the best trauma hospitals in the country. We were even closer to the Life Flight station in Mississippi, which enabled the helicopters to get to us quickly, cutting crucial minutes off our flight to the Med. In fact, that particular station was temporary; it had been set up just a few weeks before our wreck.

Atop the stack of miracles that day was the fact that the Life Flight crew had the experimental blood substitute PolyHeme on board, which was only being tested in twenty-four hospitals across the country. This was the first time that particular crew had administered it, and I believe the transfusion saved my life. (Poly-Heme still hasn't been approved by the FDA, but I pray that it will be. The flight nurses and the nurses at the Med swear by it, and I trust them completely.)

Was it a mere coincidence that the Good Samaritans who stopped to help included a preacher and his wife, Rosemary Barksdale, who comforted us and may have saved our lives with prayer, and Charika Nolan and her brother, Charles, a physical therapist who knew it was unsafe to move an accident victim and may have saved my life by keeping other people from doing so?

Coincidences? I never really believed in them. Now I know for sure that there is no such thing. I know there is something bigger than us and something great. I know it because on the day of the wreck, I saw it for myself.

People have asked me if it took me a while to remember leaving my body at the scene of the accident and going to heaven. The fact is that I remembered it right away. As soon as I opened my eyes in the ICU, after my first surgery when I was awake and in my room, I remembered. Mom had just gotten there and I thought about telling her right then. I thought about telling Holly, who was right next door to me in the ICU.

I mean, this was big news—the biggest thing that had ever happened in my life. But there was so much commotion and I was all hooked up to monitors and tubes and rods and pins. People were coming in and out of the room, and I was definitely sedated. So I waited. But I never doubted what happened. It wasn't drugs. It wasn't a dream. It was real and so comforting!

For the time being, I kept it to myself. Over the next couple of days and weeks, whenever I needed to, I just closed my eyes and went back there. In fact, I still do that.

Before the wreck, I'd heard a few "life-after-death" or "near-death" experience stories, mostly in church. I'd heard a few stories about angels appearing to people on earth. Although they are incredible stories, for the most part, I believed them. After all, who are we to say what does and doesn't exist? But I'd never really paid attention to the details when I was eighteen or twenty-two or twenty-six. I never thought this would happen to me anytime soon.

Then, when I was recovering from the accident, I read the best-selling book *90 Minutes in Heaven* by the Baptist minister Don Piper. I was blown away by his experience.

Back in January of 1989, Piper was driving on a bridge in Texas when he was hit head-on by an 18-wheeler. His car was crushed and he died instantly. When the rescue squad reached the scene, they declared him dead and covered him with a tarp. A Good Samaritan, who coincidentally (or not so coincidentally) was also a preacher, stopped to help, and even though the EMTs told him that Piper was dead, the man prayed for Piper and refused to leave him. Despite the fact that his body was virtually shattered and his heart had stopped for over ninety minutes,

Piper was revived and lived to tell about an amazing trip to heaven. His story has inspired thousands of people, including me.

There are many differences between my story and Don Piper's. For starters, his injuries were much worse than mine. What that poor man went through!

Significantly, Piper was declared dead whereas I was not. Technically, I was in hemorrhagic shock following sudden and rapid loss of significant amounts of blood. If I hadn't gotten a transfusion when I did, I would have died at the scene. Piper was also in heaven much longer than I was. But despite these different details, as I read his book, I was amazed to discover the common threads of our experiences.

When our spirits left our bodies, we both experienced no sense of time. We both felt an enormous sense of peace, saw gorgeous, indescribable scenery, and heard sublime music. We both saw loved ones and relatives who had passed away, all of whom seemed to be greeting us to take us on a journey. We both felt guided by a gorgeous light, a presence, which in my case, felt like a female presence, although I never saw an actual face or body.

I have since read more about the topic of life after death. There are several famous doctors, including Raymond Moody and Elisabeth Kübler-Ross, who have spent years interviewing people who claim to have died and gone to heaven. Moody published *Life after Life* in the mid-'70s, and it's still in print, having been updated several times. In Moody's book, there is, again, similarity between the accounts, regardless of the storyteller's background, age, sex, or religion. I was particularly interested in the fact that so many people recounted how the experience freed them from focusing on their physical body. This has been true for me and it has been a great gift. Knowing that the spirit matters more than the body—I mean really knowing it—has helped free me from being self-conscious about scars, lumps, the marks from a skin graft, or the fact that one of my legs is now shorter than the other.

Sure, I have my moments. There is a huge protruding lump over my ankle, and when I saw myself limping down the aisle on my sister's wedding video, I wanted to hide from the world. But I truly feel less self-conscious about my body than I did as a teenager or a woman in my twenties. How great is that?

Many people consider the subject of death to be taboo. I certainly never was comfortable talking about it before the accident. Even now, I don't go around telling people that I "died." For the first few weeks and months after the accident, I was reluctant to tell anyone about my experience. When I told Mom about it—I'm not saying she doubted me, as anyone would have questions—but the first thing she said was, "Are you sure?"

Then when she heard the medical staff say, "We lost her" or "She was gone" when talking about my condition after the accident and before I got the PolyHeme, Mom knew. I wasn't hallucinating. I wasn't dreaming. There was a heaven.

I wanted to share the story with others, but I worried that people would think I was crazy or on drugs. But then, as the weeks went on, whenever I talked to someone who had been in a bad accident, it always seemed as though we were both tip-toeing around the subject and wanted to share. Then, one of us would.

It was easier for me to share my story with people of faith. I found them to be the most receptive to hearing what I'd experienced. And to answer the question everyone asks: Yes, it has made me no longer afraid of death.

Which is not to say I didn't have some dark moments. I don't remember saying this, but one night, when I was in a lot of pain, I said to my mom, "I wish I was dead!" I don't think I really wanted to die. I just wanted the pain to stop. The thing was, though, that I wasn't afraid of dying. I'd already died and it was beautiful. It was comforting to know that my grandparents and all that peace and joy and love was waiting for me on the other side. But I wasn't ready to go back there just yet.

Chapter 6

Almost Home

I was really lucky that in the beginning, I had no idea what was coming. If I had known that ultimately I would have fourteen surgeries in Memphis and nine more down the road, I would have sunk into a very deep funk. Maybe it was the painkillers, which helped keep my brain from spinning. Or maybe I was just so happy to be alive and so busy simply sleeping, breathing, and living that I didn't waste time contemplating all the worst-case scenarios.

I trusted the doctors, and I had a lot of them: trauma docs, orthopedic docs, endocrinologists, and plastic surgeons. I also trusted all the nurses, the X-ray techs, and the anesthesiologists. These people made me feel that everything was going to be all right.

After about two weeks in the ICU, Dr. Croce said I could be moved to another floor. Although I was still going in and out of surgery and still needed constant care, I no longer needed to be within the very intense confines of the ICU.

I can't say enough good things about the people in the critical care unit of the Med. Not only did they save my life, but they were also so kind and loving to me and my family. I knew I would miss the people, but I would not miss the ICU.

No one likes being in an emergency room. It's tense and loud; I could hear the helicopters landing and taking off, which caused me to flashback repeatedly to the day of the accident. Every time someone was brought in, I would hear the sounds of equipment being shuttled back and forth, along with loud voices, and sometimes, I would hear screams. Although I truly felt for the patients being admitted there (I always wondered what happened to them and prayed that they would be all right), it was really, really stressful. There was a woman in the room next to me who was in a full body cast and she couldn't stop moaning. She must have been in terrible pain, but that sound—I still can't get it out of my head.

When you're in critical condition, the very necessary twenty-four-hour care you receive doesn't allow for much rest. Nurses constantly wake you up to take your blood pressure, take your temperature, draw blood, adjust your catheter or your ventilator, and, in my case, test my blood sugar or adjust my insulin drip. They come in to help you use the bed pan—which I greatly appreciated—or to change your bandages or to move you so you don't get bedsores. For someone who was supposed to be lying around, it seemed as if I never stopped moving.

When Dr. Croce said I could "step down" to another floor, I was really glad. But when he said I'd be moving to the burn unit, I didn't know what to think. As it turned out, it was a wonderful thing. First of all, it was much quieter. Secondly, I had a private room, which was big enough that, if necessary, Mom could stay in there with me. It really helped me having her nearby.

By the time I was moved into the burn unit, most of my visitors had left town. Dad and Holly had both gone home, although they did come back a few times. The flurry of aunts and cousins and friends had slowed down, but, as she would continue to be for months and months, Mom was always there.

Sometimes, when the pain got to be too much, Mom and I would cry together in the privacy of my new room. We prayed together a lot, too. And a couple of times, we even sang together. I remember singing that old Barry Manilow song, "I Can't Smile Without You," which cracked us all up because the truth was that I really couldn't sing. The breathing tubes had pretty much wrecked my voice, so I just kind of mouthed the words and listened to Mom sing. Once, when I was feeling really low, I asked her to sing that old hymn "I Surrender All to Thee." Mom has a beautiful, classically trained singing voice. It's so soothing. I wonder what the other patients or the nurses down the hall thought when that hymn came floating from my room that day? If I close my eyes, I can still hear that beautiful sound.

Another upside to being a patient in the burn unit was the proximity to these big, wide tables where the nurses could lay me down and give me a shower. It's difficult to find the words for how resplendent those showers were. In the ICU, I could only have a sponge bath. But in the burn unit, every few days I'd be moved to one of those tables that had a big shower head directly over top. Think of a Vichy shower in a spa! It was warm and wonderful to be underneath the water and let it run all over me. No trip to Canyon Ranch Spa could beat how amazing that felt.

Furthermore, the nurses there were so sweet. They didn't have to do as much as they did. They would wash my hair or rub lotion on me, taking extra care not to pull up the not-yet-healed scabs from where the seatbelt had cut across my waist. I'm sure I wasn't a pretty sight. Although a lot of my bruises had started to heal, I still looked like someone beat the crap out of me. I felt like a welterweight who'd gone the distance in a heavyweight fight.

You never really know what the word "humble" means until you can't leave your bed and someone has to help you go to the bathroom. Believe me, I'll never complain about a long line in the ladies' room ever again.

For much of the time I was in the hospital, I had a catheter in place, which allowed me to urinate in a bag. Other times, I would use a bedpan.

With two broken hips, a broken femur, a broken tailbone, a broken pelvis, and an external fixator holding my right leg in place, it was really difficult—not to mention painful—for the nurses to get a bedpan underneath me. What's more, sometimes the bedpan would spill in the bed, which was really uncomfortable, and one time, before someone could come in with the bedpan, I had an accident, which was so embarrassing. I just couldn't bring myself to call a nurse, so I waited until someone came in later. "You should have called," the nurse said, as he efficiently and cheerfully cleaned things up. "You don't need to be laying in this."

During the time I was in the hospital, I was mostly tube fed. I was hardly eating anything at all, and in addition to this, the medications I was taking caused me to be constipated, which was uncomfortable. On the upside, however, I didn't have to go to the bathroom as much. Finally, though, I became so uncomfortable—my stomach felt like it had rocks inside it—that I had to ask for help.

They gave me three enemas, more pills, and Milk of Magnesia. Mom and her friend even prayed over me. I did everything but eat prunes. It took a while, but finally, everything kicked in, and when it did, it was like a volcano erupting. Not fun.

Being dependent on others for my most basic needs was a huge adjustment for me, but I had no choice. I had to surrender and let people help me.

Since I was eight years old, I've been testing my own blood sugar and giving myself insulin shots for my diabetes. But while I was in the hospital, I had to let the nurses do this for me.

For one thing, I wasn't always awake or coherent enough to check my own levels. They had to check my blood sugar hourly, instead of my normal four times a day, because so many factors, such as stress, medications, and not eating, were causing my blood sugar to go haywire. Despite the fact that I was immediately put on a twenty-four-hour insulin drip, my blood sugar skyrocketed to 500 the first week I was in the hospital. The doctors couldn't manage to lower it, and I went into ketoacidosis, which occurs when the body doesn't have enough insulin and it starts using fats instead. The fat byproducts, ketones, start building up, which can lead to all sorts of problems. Some patients even slip into a coma.

I guess that should have been my primary concern, but all I could think about was how thirsty I was. I had the worst cotton mouth you can imagine, and the truly terrible part was that I couldn't drink water because of the tubes I had in my mouth. So I sucked on a little wet sponge and dreamed of waterfalls, blue lagoons, and cases of Aquafina.

I stayed on the drip the whole time I was in the hospital, and the nurses had to constantly check it and adjust the amounts. All the different medications and the stress of the surgeries caused my blood sugar to spike. Then the lack of food and all the inactivity would cause my blood sugar to drop.

It was strange to be so out of touch with what was going on in my body. Before the accident, I'd gotten so in tune with my energy levels that I could usually tell if my blood sugar was about to drop or rise without even testing my blood. Even in the middle of the night, I used to wake up automatically if my insulin dropped: I'd wake up a little weak and sweaty, and I would know.

But while I was in the hospital, if I felt sluggish, my blood sugar could have been low or it could be that one of dozens of medications was causing the dip. There was no way to know for sure. That made me extremely uneasy. My diabetes also made the doctors uneasy because, typically, people with diabetes have a more difficult time healing than regular patients. And I was a person with diabetes who'd suffered severe shock trauma and had multiple transfusions.

I didn't know this until much later, but Dr. Croce discussed his concern repeatedly with Dr. Magnotti and Dr. Fabian, especially after the surgery to repair my ruptured colon. Dr. Croce said he was pleased with the technical aspect of the surgery, but they all worried about potential leaking of my suture line.

Once again, I'm glad I didn't know about this. I didn't find out what a suture line was until later (it's the incision line), so at the time, I remained blissfully ignorant. And I would have paid any amount of money for a huge, ice-cold pitcher of lemonade.

In addition to being dependent on the kindness of people who were no longer strangers for my basic needs, I also counted on them for the extras—such as the occasional field trip. I remember the first time that a nurse got me into a special medical wheelchair—it was electric with a hard, straight back and the seat moved up and down—and rolled me outside. Yes, it hurt—a lot. But I had been in the hospital for nearly three weeks and the thought of seeing the sun was thrilling to me.

It was a beautiful, sunny day. It was probably 70 degrees. Mom walked alongside as the nurse pushed me out through the automatic doors and parked the wheelchair near the front entrance. It wasn't exactly a day at the park. In fact, the scene was a little edgy out there. Cars were pulling up out front, loud music was playing, and people were walking briskly in and out of the doorway. Maybe I would have preferred a field full of flowers as the backdrop for my first trip outside. Still, it was great. I took a long, slow, deep breath and smiled for the first time in what felt like forever.

Then, just a few minutes after we got outside, I hit the wall. My energy dipped really low and I got dizzy from sitting upright.

I knew I had to go back into my room and get back into bed. But that was all right. I knew I'd be outside again soon. And if that was true, then Coronas on the beach couldn't be far behind.

Not to take away from my broken hips and crushed thigh bone, but my grisliest injury was probably the open distal tibia fracture— or, in other words, the hole in my leg just above my ankle. It makes my stomach turn just thinking about it, but at least the hole, which was open for about ten days, was covered with dressings and sterile bandages until it could be permanently closed.

As with most of my surgeries, the hole had to be addressed in steps. First, there was an exploratory surgery for the plastic surgeon to evaluate the wound and also to check for infection and other problems. Then, the surgeons did a skin graft, where they took skin from my butt to make a flap. For a long time after that, it felt like someone dragged a cheese grater across my backside. Next, they affixed the fifteen-centimeter long by ten-centimeter wide flap to my leg, effectively covering the hole by cauterizing, stitching, and stapling a permanent trap door into place. During the surgeries, the external fixator was loosened and removed from my leg, but as soon as they were done, they put the bars back on and retightened the clamps. I couldn't wait to be free of that thing.

The skin flap procedures were my last surgeries in Memphis. They saved this for last because once you start a skin graft, you don't want to cut through it. It needs time to heal. So by that point, everything that could be done had been done. During the last few weeks, they'd checked almost everything off their list, going back to tighten this screw or put in another bolt that they may have not gotten a chance to put in place because an earlier operation was cut short.

I was at a point where there was nothing to do but wait.

So instead of sitting around in Memphis while everyone waited to see what did and didn't heal properly, Dr. Croce decided I could be transferred to Vanderbilt Hospital in Nashville, which was not only in my hometown, but was a top-notch orthopedic center where the upcoming and, as it turned out, very complicated surgeries could be performed.

On April 12, I was deemed stable enough to move. At first, they were going to move me to Nashville by ambulance, but Dr. Croce said that he did not recommend this mode of transportation for the two-hundred-plus-mile trip. "It's going to be a really bumpy ride," he said. "And you'll be hurting."

So once my insurance approved payment for transportation by medical jet, we started preparations for the flight. I was so happy to be going home. Or close to home, anyway. But of course I had mixed feelings about leaving the people who had taken such good care of me. I'd gotten so close to the doctors, such as Dr. Perez, my orthopedic doctor, and Dr. Croce, who oversaw my case. I trusted them and I was a little apprehensive about starting all over in a new place.

A couple of doctors and nurses admitted that they were sorry to see me go, too. We'd formed a bond; they saved my life and watched me progress from touch-and-go to getting better every day. I felt a little guilty leaving them. I wondered if the Memphis staff felt like the guy who drives eleven hours for a weekend at the shore, and during the last half-hour of the all-night trip, his friend, who had been sleeping the entire way, takes the wheel and triumphantly pulls up in front of the beach house and shouts, "We're here!"

Anyway, after a few teary goodbyes and hours of discharge paperwork later, several orderlies came into my room to lift me from my bed to a stretcher by pulling up the sheet underneath me and turning it into a makeshift hammock. I would have thought it was funny, maybe even fun, being swung that way if it didn't hurt so much.

Next, I was wheeled out on the stretcher to the waiting medical jet, which was a tiny private plane, much like the ones my dad flies on, except instead of a bench or seats, there was space for a stretcher. When they locked the stretcher in place and Mom climbed on board behind me, it was almost 10:00 at night.

I was lying down, so I couldn't see outside, but I remember Mom looking out the windows and breathing a sigh of relief. "Look at all those stars!" she said. "It's so beautiful! We'll be home soon."

I'm not sure why we took off so late. I think that transferring all the records and making last-minute arrangements was complicated. What's more, the coordinator who was helping us said we had only a short window of opportunity to leave, per the insurance company's instructions. By the time we landed in Nashville and I was transported by ambulance to Vanderbilt Hospital, it was close to midnight.

I expected to feel a huge sense of relief when we rolled into Vanderbilt, a place I'd been several times before as a patient and a visitor. I'd driven by this hospital thousands of times. It was just a few miles from my house, and my friends and Holly would be able to visit me anytime. In fact, Holly was already there waiting for me in my room, which she was fixing up for my arrival.

There were so many positives to being in Nashville. It's close to Dad's house, so he could bring Katie and Sam over. Thinking about all these things should have made me happy. Earlier in the day, I was excited about the trip. I thought, once I get to Nashville, everything will be better. But looking back, I must have set my expectations way too high, because the moment I was brought into my nice, clean, bright, private room, this dark cloud of disappointment descended on me. I kept thinking,

"I'm not home. I'm never going to get home. This is starting all over again. I hurt worse today than I did two weeks ago . . . " I just couldn't stop my thoughts from swirling. I tried to calm down and convince myself that I was simply exhausted. I knew Mom was about to collapse, too, so I told her and Holly to go home. And I meant it.

I didn't blame either of them for wanting to leave, especially Mom. She was running on empty. She hadn't been to her house in over four weeks. She must have been dying to unpack, change clothes, pick up mail, and, most of all, sleep in her own bed.

So they both left, promising to come back first thing in the morning, and I tried to go to sleep. But the pain wouldn't let me. I'd gotten some painkillers, but the jostling around during the trip must have been too much. So I just laid there in the dark, quiet room, wincing and staring up at the ceiling.

Then, much to my surprise, an hour later, a group of doctors walked into my room. They were led by Dr. Philip Kregor, Director of Orthopedic Trauma, who made a beeline for my chart hanging at the foot of my bed. He picked it up and read it carefully, flipping back and forth between the pages. Then he looked up at me with this very intense look on his face and said, "You're going to need another surgery."

Then he and the other doctors turned and walked out.

I shouldn't have been surprised. I knew that I would need more surgeries, but the thought of another one right away hit me like a water balloon on a freezing cold day.

Dr. Kregor was all business that night. He wasted no time on pleasantries such as "How are you, Hilary?" In my case, that was a dumb question anyway. He knew how I was. I was broken. And his job was to figure out how to fix me.

Looking back, I can totally understand his lack of small talk. It must have been a stressful situation for him. Look at the case he was inheriting. Even though he had all the records and information from the doctors in Memphis, he was essentially starting from scratch. He had to make some huge decisions about my care and he had to make them very quickly. There was a lot of information to weigh. Years later, I can say I truly love this man. We have been through a lot and I am grateful for all he's done for me. I've come to appreciate his straightforward manner. And now that things aren't so serious, we laugh and joke a lot. But that night, things just hit me wrong.

Everything would have been fine if I'd gone right to sleep, but I couldn't. Then, I started feeling anxious because I hardly ever have trouble falling asleep.

Why is it that when you try really hard to fall asleep, you just can't? It's like the night before you go on a trip where you can't fall asleep because you keep obsessing about the fact that you have to get up early to catch the plane and if you don't sleep, you're going to be tired or maybe oversleep and miss the flight. Then you really can't sleep.

It was a lot like that, only worse, because the pain was just throbbing and I couldn't put it out of my mind. So it grew and grew like a ripple in a pond that just keeps growing into a bigger and bigger circle. The pain was amplified by the quiet in my room. For a long time, no one came in the room, which was different from what I was used to. In Memphis, especially in the ICU, nurses came into my room nonstop. But in Nashville, I was in a regular orthopedic unit. Nurses wouldn't be coming in nonstop anymore. Be careful what you wish for, right? In Memphis, I sometimes wished everyone would just leave me alone so I could sleep. Now, I was all alone and hurting badly, and it was causing me to panic. So I grabbed my phone and called Holly, who had just gotten home and climbed into bed. "Holly, no one's here!" I said. "I'm in so much pain. I'm all alone." Then I started bawling and couldn't stop. "Another surgery! I can't believe I have to have another surgery!"

Holly listened as I cried and cried. She listened and tried to calm me down. "We'll be there first thing," she promised. "It's all going to be okay."

Neither Holly nor Mom realized that I would be alone most of that first night. They both say they feel guilty about not staying with me, which makes me feel bad. (Everyone feels bad about everyone else feeling bad. Do we need therapy, or what?) They both made it up to me in a big way. For the duration of my hospital stay, I was never alone again.

When morning came, things definitely started getting better. The best thing happened my second day in the Nashville hospital when Dr. Kregor took the external fixator off my leg. Of course that same day he also surgically inserted a plate into my ankle, but even though I couldn't jump up and down or even get out of bed yet, I felt free. Think of getting your braces off or getting a cast removed, then multiply it by forty. No more big, metal contraption clamping down and sticking through my leg in four different places. It felt fantastic!

Then, just as I'd looked forward to, my friends started to come and visit. One of the first people I saw was Tony Armani. During the last week or so I was in the hospital in Memphis, Tony was also in the hospital at St. Thomas in Nashville. After having chest pains and breathing problems that were wrongly diagnosed as asthma, Tony found out he had congestive heart failure and landed in the hospital. As he tells the story, when he started to suspect something was really wrong, he called his doctor and said, "Is it normal for my ankles to be the size of my calves?"

He was the last person I talked to before the wreck. I remember him saying, "Be careful!" right before we hung up.

By the time I moved to Vanderbilt, Tony was home recuperating. He wasn't supposed to be up and around, but he came to visit me anyway. The minute I saw his face, I felt better. Not only is Tony an incredibly talented artist and musician, but he's just an uplifting person to be around. And it's not just his warm personality and killer English accent. The guy is buoyant!

A few months before my accident, I visited Tony at his house/studio where he was preparing for an upcoming art show. While he was working, I flopped down on a settee in the room and stretched out with one of my legs dangling over the side. My phone rang and I took the call, so it took me a few minutes to notice that Tony had grabbed some loose paper and was sketching away. He loved the red boots I was wearing and they inspired him to draw a picture of my right leg. He finished the sketch and went into his room and started painting right away. Later, when the painting was complete, he framed it with copper and set it aside.

Tony put the painting in the art show, which opened not long after the car wreck, but as he hung it, a sinking feeling came over him when he noticed the image of my right leg—the leg that was broken in so many places and at the time was being held together by a stainless steel rod. He just couldn't bring himself to sell the painting, so he put a "SOLD" sign on it and saved it for me. As he put it, "You had to have your leg back!"

I love that painting, which still hangs in my living room. But I tease Tony that I'm not sure I want to be his subject anymore. After all, he painted a series of hearts before his own congestive heart disease diagnosis—another example of the power of visualization. Beware of your dominant thoughts!

Other visitors came to see me at Vanderbilt, including my dad's booking agent and friends who I knew from college. Sam and Katie came and brought me presents, including a new pair of pajamas that I couldn't wait to wear. I perked up when musician friends, including Laurie Webb and Bobby Tomberlin, the songwriter who wrote "One More Day," came to see me. It made me really look forward to getting back into music.

I'm glad that in Nashville, there wasn't a paparazzi problem or any tabloid drama like what my family encountered in Memphis. I'm sure part of the reason was that the critical element was gone: I hadn't just been in a life-threatening wreck. I guess "Hank Junior's Daughter in the Hospital for Treatment of Complex Orthopedic Injuries" is a less sensational headline than "Hank Junior's Daughters Near Death Following Horrific Wreck."

Another reason I think things were calmer is that people in Nashville are used to seeing country music celebrities and, for the most part, leave them alone. People see Kenny Chesney eating lunch or Alan Jackson stopped at a stoplight, and usually no one freaks out. So when Dad came to the hospital in Nashville, there wasn't a lot of commotion.

Just to be safe, because the security was looser (Detective Dan had moved on to new adventures), I was admitted under the alias "Samantha Colt." I'm not sure why we used that name, but only friends and family knew about it, and that seemed to keep out unwanted guests—for the most part.

There was, however, one small incident in which a woman, someone who worked at the hospital, wandered into my room one day and sat down in the chair by the window. "I can't believe you're Hank Williams's granddaughter!" she said. "How is that possible . . . I just love Hank Jr.'s music . . . " She went on and on for about thirty minutes until, to my great relief, a nurse came in and she got up and left. I never saw her again.

When I was brought into Vanderbilt, I was off the feeding tube, and even though I still didn't have much of an appetite, now I could eat regular food. The bad news was, well, let's just say, that I learned that I had to bring my own lunch—or someone in my family would bring me sushi or Subway or Italian food from Valentino's. I've never figured out why hospital food can't be a little better. I understand that the cafeteria workers are cooking for a lot of people. But healing patients should eat whole grains and lean protein and fresh fruit and steamed veggies. If I ever see another Salisbury steak with gravy and white bread, it will be too soon.

Also, what about the hospital gowns? I understand that it's necessary for patients to wear loose, open clothing so the nurses and doctors can have easy access. But do they have to look and feel the way they do?

Here's my idea for a new product: soft, reasonably attractive hospital gowns that close all the way in the back. Instead of string ties, these gowns will attach and easily unattach with snaps or Velcro. And the gowns will be made from fun, colorful fabrics—maybe paisley or leopard prints.

I told Dr. Kregor my idea and he loves it. See? We did get to be friends. We both think a doctor's office should be more like a spa. I always had my iPod with me so I could pop in my earphones and play relaxing music anytime. And because I wasn't in the ICU anymore, people could bring me flowers or I would bring in items like jars of reeds scented with aromatherapy oils. I remember the nurses walking in and saying, "What smells so good in here?"

Everyone took it as a good sign that I was thinking about things like frumpy hospital gowns or laughing at the pancakes on my morning breakfast tray, joking that if I'd wanted to, I could have used them to really hurt someone. But even though my spirits were up, I still had a long way to go.

As the doctors discussed which bones or body parts they would try to fix next, I was left to wonder what this all meant. I never came out and asked the question, "Will I walk again?" because I just had faith that I would. I knew it would take several surgeries and a lot of time. I knew that I wouldn't exactly be able to sprint or even strut—not at first, anyway.

It's a cliché, but for me it was really true: one step at a time.

Chapter 7

Opposites

People often ask me if there was music in our house when I was growing up. There was. But not the way you might think.

Mom was a music major in college. She's a classically trained pianist and has a beautiful voice; she even played the part of Maria in her sorority's production of *The Sound of Music*. But as it turned out, she never sought out a career as a musician. Although she sang professionally a few times (that's her singing the high harmony on the 1978 Waylon Jennings/Willie Nelson song "Mamas Don't Let Your Babies Grow Up to Be Cowboys." When Waylon said, "We can't find a backup singer," Dad replied, "Becky can do it"), she never pursued singing full time.

She did sing around the house, though, and she still does. She would sing while cooking dinner or folding laundry or she would sit at the piano at night and play and sing. She sang in church—we all did that—and recently, she did backup vocals on some of my demos and on Holly's 2009 album, *Here With Me*.

When I was little, Dad gave me a set of drums one Christmas. He also gave me an omnichord, which is a kind of keyboard instrument that makes really weird sounds. In fact, I still have it and Holly used it on one of her records.

I remember Dad had guitars all over the house, and sometimes he would sit around strumming one of those guitars and humming or singing a little. Sometimes he'd sit with me or Holly at the piano or he and Mom would sit there and play. There's a great clip of them from a *20/20* TV special from the early '80s, where they're sitting at the piano singing Waylon and Jessi's song "Storms Never Last."

But back then, and even later when we were in junior high and high school and he would visit us, I never saw him come blasting in the room playing "White Lightning" or some Marshall Tucker Band cover song. Okay, once Mom had to scold him for playing "Buck Nekkid" for us, and he did play the piano with his boot a couple of times. He even tried to show me how to do it— "You just do this and this and this . . . "—but I never really got the hang of it.

Mostly, though, the music he or we played at home was more mellow. Even after my parents split, he would always leave a guitar at the house so he could play when he came over. But as far as we were concerned, in our house, he was just Dad—not Bocephus.

It's funny, too, when people assume that we constantly had Hank Williams, Sr.'s music playing in our house, like some sort of family soundtrack. I probably shouldn't admit this, but I don't ever remember hearing a Hank Williams record or anybody playing or singing a Hank Williams song in our house when I was young. Although I absolutely love my grandfather's music now and appreciate his incredible songwriting, when I was little, his music kind of bored me.

When you're a teenager, you want upbeat, fun music (unless your "crush" is ignoring you!), and in our day it was Mariah Carey or George Michael or New Kids on the Block. Later, in high school, my tastes changed a bit, so I loved listening to the Spice Girls, Stone Temple Pilots, Pearl Jam, Nirvana, Janet Jackson, and Michael Jackson. After that it was Sheryl Crow, Sarah McLachlan, Fleetwood Mac, Aerosmith, and the Rolling Stones. But when I eleven, twelve, and thirteen, it was all about New Kids on the Block. I even had a New Kids sleeping bag, board game, and slippers. I had a New Kids pillow case and slept with it every night.

When I turned twelve, my friends, in cahoots with Mom and Holly, threw me a surprise party. My friend Shanna took me shopping to get me out of the house. We went to Merle Norman Cosmetics, and I remember this lady putting eye shadow on me for my birthday makeover. Then we went back to my house and when we walked in, everybody jumped out and yelled, "Surprise!" Somebody put on a New Kids on the Block tape, and then Mom brought out a birthday cake decorated with red roses and a record album with "New Kids on the Block" spelled out in icing.

We were so in love with those guys. Joe was Holly's favorite. She had a poster of him in her room and kissed it so many times she wore a hole in it. Jonathan was my guy. I was sure that he and his bandmates were singing, "Be My Girl" or "Stop It Girl" or "Please Don't Go Girl" about me.

Of course, as every teenage girl from the early '90s knows, New Kids reunited in 2008. Maybe it's not the same seeing these five guys when they're pushing forty and we're pushing thirty, but my friends and I went to that show. Shanna always wanted to meet Jordan Knight. In fact, when we were kids, she used to say, "I'm going to work with him someday."

Almost twenty years after my New Kids birthday party, Jordan was in Nashville working on a solo album. Shanna knew his manager, and one day, he invited Shanna to the studio where Jordan was recording and introduced her to him. They talked, and Jordan said he was thinking about touring the country to recruit talented fans to sing on his new solo album or to open for some of his shows. So Shanna started working as the booker for that talent search, called Jordan Idol.

I told her, see, that's proof that when you put it out there in the universe, then it comes back to you. Shanna (being Shanna) said, "Well, I don't know about that. I also put it out in the universe that I liked this particular guy and nothing happened."

I told her that even the universe knows that some things aren't meant to be.

Growing up, life was pretty ordinary for Holly and me. On weekdays, we'd go to school, and then when we came home in the afternoon, Mom would make us a snack. She'd toast up cheese tortillas with salsa and we'd watch *Mickey Mouse Club*, *Full House*, or *The Brady Bunch* before we went upstairs to do our homework. Some days we'd go to piano lessons or voice lessons or Holly would go to gymnastics.

Every night, the three of us ate dinner together and, before we went to bed, Mom had us read devotionals from our Precious Moments children's Bible, like the story of Jonah and the Whale or Noah's Ark.

On the weekends, we'd wake up and Mom would make us pancakes. Then we'd go play putt-putt golf or ice skating or bowling. Unless we were on our death beds, we went to church every Sunday. In the summer, we took trips to the beach or to Dollywood in East Tennessee with Mom's family, and then over Easter and Christmas breaks we'd go visit my grandparents and cousins and aunts and uncles in Louisiana.

Our house was always really clean and tidy; Mom kept it that way. It's embarrassing for me to say this now, but even when we were in high school, Holly and I didn't do a lot of chores around the house. We didn't do laundry and we hardly ever cooked. Mom considered housework to be her domain, although we were supposed to keep our rooms clean. I did pretty well with that, but Holly's room was legendary for its chaos.

I guess housework wasn't a priority to us because we were far too busy planning our annual fashion shows. Every year, Holly,

Shanna, and, one year, our friend Sarah and I produced and videotaped a fashion show, complete with an original theme. One of the standouts was Fun in the Sun '91, which featured all of us modeling summer clothes down the "runway" (a.k.a. the living room) with Beach Boys music—*Aruba, Jamaica, oooh I wanna take ya*—blaring in the background.

We didn't worry too much with the sets; we chose to focus on the clothes and the talent part of the program, where we'd interview each other as if we were on *Entertainment Tonight*. At the end of the video, the music would play on—*Come on pretty mama*—as we held up cards for the credits: Producer: Holly Williams.

Another time, we made a video where, for some bizarre reason, Tom Cruise and Christie Brinkley were getting married. (Holly played the part of Tom, and I played the part of Christie.) I wore one of mom's dresses and we did a whole wedding thing. Some girls look at *Brides* magazine; we made videos.

For the most part, Holly and I got along really well when we were growing up. It's kind of amazing that we did (and still do), considering that we are polar opposites. Holly is outgoing, fearless, and loud. I'm shy, reserved, and quiet. Holly sprints from the car to the dry cleaners or the drug store. Me? Even before I walked with a cane, I took my time.

Holly bursts into someone's house and opens their refrigerator door and helps herself. She'll tell people her life story the day she meets them. Things just fly out of her mouth. Me? Once I get to know someone, I'm really talkative, but at first, I watch my choice of words. It takes me a minute to warm up to people.

Up until I was about seventeen, when we were both in high school and hanging out with our own friends, Holly and I were together all the time. And of course Mom was there, too. We really were the Three Musketeers—until the fights broke out. Then Holly and I were the boxers at center ring and Mom was the referee.

When I was eleven years old, Dad gave Holly and me each a ring—one of those watch rings. One day, I saw Holly wearing mine even though she had one of her own. I got so mad that I punched her in the nose. That was one of the few times I remember Dad calling to speak to me when I was in trouble; Mom had called him for backup. I remember trembling when I picked up the phone. "Hilary," he said. "We're too big to be punching people. You don't need to do that anymore."

Mostly, the fights Holly and I had were pretty minor and didn't last very long. And the fights were almost always about clothes. Specifically, they were about Holly, my younger sister, borrowing and not returning and sometimes even losing my clothes, earrings, shoes, and so forth. The biggest fight I can remember was the Prada Purse Fight of 2000. Holly was going to New York for Winterim, a high school field trip, and wanted to take my purse with her to the big city. I'd saved up my money for months to buy this purse I'd spotted at Neiman Marcus. It was the perfect black, over-the-shoulder Prada bag. I was afraid she'd lose it, so I said, "No way. You're not taking it."

Well, Holly is hardheaded (as I can be, too), and she wants what she wants when she wants it. "Yes, I am taking it, Hilary!"

She grabbed the purse and started to walk away. Then I stood up, reached around her, and grabbed onto the strap, but she wouldn't let go. We were both yelling and pulling on this $250 purse, back and forth like it was a piece of rope in a tug-of-war. I can still see her boyfriend just standing there with his eyes all wide, like, Get me out of here! Then Mom came in and said, "Hilary, c'mon now! Just give it to her."

Well, Holly took the purse to New York. And to my shock and amazement, she returned it to me after she came back. It did take her about a week or so, but at least I got it back intact.

Looking back, though, fighting was the exception, not the rule. Mostly, my sister and I stuck together. So during tough times or awkward times, we were a team. Like when Mom decided to teach us about the birds and the bees.

We were young—I was eleven and Holly was nine—so we were pretty squirrely about the topic. And poor Mom! Even though we were all girls and we were really close, she was struggling with how to go about it. So she got out a book. Basically, it was a manual for conceiving and having a baby. It was very technical with lots of pictures. She sat us down in the playroom and read the entire book to us, page by page. Holly and I were so embarrassed. "Mom," I said. "We really don't want to hear about this!"

Mom is a very dedicated Christian, so she did her best to guide us according to her beliefs. "Girls," she said. "God says we need to respect our bodies because they're his. You need to save yourself for marriage."

What she was saying was about as relevant to the lives of an eleven-year-old girl and her hyper younger sister as the pictures in the book. But we knew her heart was in the right place. It was just awkward.

I guess every parent is uncomfortable with talking about this stuff. Years later, when Katie got her period, Dad called me and asked me to talk to her. "Katie's going through the change of life," he said. "Can you talk to her about, ya' know, female things?"

As far as Mom goes, her attitudes have changed and evolved over the years. How could they not, with her raising two teenage daughters in the 1990s, with one (guess who?) telling her everything under the sun? Still, it's funny, even now, when we go to movies together, she'll freak out when a couple is making out on screen.

I wouldn't say that Mom was an authoritarian parent. She let us do a lot of fun things and was pretty open-minded, but she was very strict regarding the music we listened to. She was well aware of our obsession with New Kids on the Block, which she thought was fine, until she saw Donnie Wahlberg grab his crotch during one of their videos and she flipped out. She must have been having a bad day, because as soon as she saw that, she took one of our New Kids cassette tapes and smashed it to bits with a hammer! After that, watching MTV or VH1 was out.

If there was music we liked of which she didn't approve (George Michael and Janet Jackson's "nasty" lyrics were forbidden), we'd just sneak it into the house like contraband. That worked for a while until, one day, she found a bunch of my CDs and read the lyrics on the liner notes. She must have thrown away fifty CDs—Stone Temple Pilots, Pearl Jam, Nirvana . . . all gone! I was not happy about that.

From then on, she insisted on reading the lyrics of any CD we brought home. When the band Bush were coming to Nashville for a concert, Holly and I really wanted to go see them, but we knew they would never pass the lyrics test. So Holly took one of her Christian music CDs, cut out their lyrics, and pasted them on top of the words to the songs on the Bush CD. Brilliant! Mom let us go to the show.

Even though we lived in Music City and were Hank Jr.'s daughters, we really didn't go to many concerts even when we were a little older. Part of it was the fact that there were only so many Christian CDs that Holly could cut and paste, and part of it was that Dad didn't want us to go. I guess he'd seen enough of what went on out in the crowd and especially backstage to know he didn't want his young daughters hanging around. It's funny, but the few concerts we went to seemed very tame to me. We just had a good time.

Still, we didn't go very often, even to Dad's shows. The late '80s, specifically '87–'89, were the years he was named Entertainer of the Year by both the Academy of Country Music and the

Country Music Association. He was at the top of his game and his shows were wild, with him running around with his shirt off, jumping up on pianos, and shooting off guns.

When I was only four or five years old, I remember going to one of his concerts, where Holly and I sat in director's chairs off to the side of the stage and watched the show. At one point, he introduced us to the crowd, and then later, he came over and sang to us. I was really embarrassed. But what I remember most was that all these women in the crowd and standing around the side of the stage were wearing those really high-waisted jeans that were in style back then. They tied their plaid shirts up in a knot under their boobs and bared their midriffs. Holly and I thought that was hilarious.

When we were in high school, we went to one or two of his shows every year. He'd always make these occasions really special, sometimes surprising us by sending a limo to pick us up and then we'd fly to the show on his private plane. Those were the best days; Holly and I felt like we'd won the lottery!

Once, when we got on the plane, he had boxes waiting for us with brand new cowboy boots and fringe jackets with big shoulder pads. That's what we get for making fun of the women in the high-waisted jeans.

Of course, we saw Dad more than once or twice a year at his shows. We almost always saw him over Christmas, and he was great about showing up for our birthdays or calling us, at the very least. He brought us the best presents from the road. One year, he brought us a real vintage pinball machine, and I thought it was the coolest thing ever. Other times, we would go and visit him at his home in Paris, Tennessee, about two hours outside of Nashville, or at his cabin in Montana. The first time we went to visit Dad in Montana, I was nine years old. Holly and I flew out there on the plane by ourselves (with an airline escort). Holly, who was only seven at the time, was really attached to Mom. She was attached to her at the hip, and this was our first time we would be away from Mom—far away where we couldn't run home to her—so Holly clung to me the entire time.

We learned early on that we'd see our dad more if we were willing to do things that he wanted to do. Holly and I are city girls, or maybe it's more accurate to say we are "indoor girls." We prefer shopping or getting our nails done to sitting in duck blinds, but Dad loves to hunt and fish. So in order to spend time with him, sometimes we'd go hunting and fishing. From the time I was four years old, I'd ask Dad to take me hunting or fishing. Usually, we'd go fishing, something kid-friendly, like bream fishing on a small lake. And occasionally, he'd let us shoot at cans or targets in his yard, where he has a whole bunch of metal chickens and pigs set up. Then, finally, when I was fourteen years old, he decided Holly and I were old enough to go deer hunting. He loves to tell the story about our first trip.

Neither of us liked getting up early, but one Saturday while visiting him in Paris, Tennessee, Dad woke us up before sunrise and we grumpily rolled out of bed and headed out to his favorite deer stand. It was a nice one, kind of like a tree house, and we climbed up into it while it was still dark and sat down in folding chairs on either side of him. It was cold out there, and really quiet. We got tired just sitting there so we kept falling asleep. "C'mon girls," Dad said. "You have to watch! You have to be ready."

Then he showed us how to aim and shoot our guns. Holly thought it was weird that we weren't seeing any deer, so she put down her gun and decided to do something to help. "Go deer! Go deer!" she yelled, putting on her best cheerleading moves.

Dad was gesturing wildly. "Shhhhhhhhhhhhhhhhh! Holly! Quiet!"

"Why do I have to be quiet?" she said, practicing her splits.

Incredibly, despite the commotion, a buck had wandered into the clearing. I took aim and shot. Missed! Right over its head. As the deer scampered away, Dad showed me again how to use the scope and told me next time, go straight for the heart. After an hour or two, another buck, this one a seven-pointer, came into sight. I took aim and shot. This time, I hit him and he went down right away.

"Whoa!" Dad said, putting down his gun. "Let's go, Hilary!"

As we climbed out of the stand, my heart was pounding. First of all, the gun shot scared me; I was using a .30-06, and it kicked back hard when I shot. Second, even though I was happy about making the shot and Dad seemed so proud, I felt bad about killing the deer. "That deer had a broken leg," Dad told me, when he saw my long face. "Deer can't live with a broken leg. He had to be shot."

Dad took the deer home, hung it up, and processed the meat, which we ate a few weeks later.

We've been hunting a few times since, despite the fact that one time Dad had to send me back to take a shower (I was wearing perfume) and spray me down with Scent Lock before we hit the stand. But nothing compares to that first trip. A girl never forgets her first buck.

When I got to be in my twenties, if I met someone and they found out my Dad was Hank Williams, Jr., more often than not they'd say, "Man, I can only imagine what your house was like when you were a kid!"

They were picturing the "All My Rowdy Friends Are Coming Over Tonight" video or the introduction to Monday Night Football. They would have been so disappointed to see the actual scene. Instead of Willie Nelson or Kris Kristofferson tapping a keg, it was me, Mom, and Holly sitting around the house having potluck dinners with friends from our church group. George Jones never drove drunk across our lawn on his riding lawn mower—that we know of. If he did, we missed it because we were sitting in our bean bag chairs playing Monopoly.

Although she'll have the occasional glass of wine or cocktail, Mom never really drank. And the whole time I was growing up, I never saw Dad drunk at home. He'll have some wine or beer now and then, but growing up, he never drank around us. I don't think I saw him have a beer until I was out of high school.

I know he drank—and drank plenty—on the road. He never told us these stories, but we'd hear from different people such as Cowboy, his steel guitar player, about how, back in the '70s, the band would sometimes party for days. They'd go AWOL, and because there were no cell phones or pagers back then, the people from the record company would have to get on a plane and fly to the city where they were playing and search every bar until they found the guys in the band and drag them to the venue.

Although Dad tried to protect us when he was around, sometimes people at concerts or out and about in Nashville—usually people I didn't know—would make it their business to tell me that they'd seen him drinking or partying or doing this or that. It made me uncomfortable; it still does. I don't know why people feel compelled to tell me this stuff. I mean, don't they realize he's my Dad?

Holly usually lets it roll off her back, even when some random woman comes up to her after one of her shows and says, "Oh, hi. Your dad knows me as Candy. I knew him back in the day." She just shakes her head and says, "Gee, thanks for telling me that."

I have to work a little harder not to let it bother me.

At the risk of sounding like a daughter in denial, I really don't think Dad is or ever was an alcoholic. Mom and Holly say the same thing. He had his battles with pills in the '70s when he was sinking into a deep depression, and he partied—like most big entertainers did in the '80s. But he never struggled with drug addiction like his dear friends Johnny Cash and Waylon Jennings. He never went to rehab.

It's ironic, but because my stepmom has struggled with sobriety and addiction off and on over the years, he is often the responsible parent in his house. On Sundays, he likes to drink beer and watch football. But most days, he's a regular dad, taking my sister Katie and my brother Sam to their soccer games.

This is the polar opposite of how Dad grew up. When he was little, there were constant parties going on in the living room, many of them featuring very famous guests. When he was just five or six years old, people like Jerry Lee Lewis and Fats Domino used to sit him down and teach him how to play the piano. People would take turns teaching him guitar licks or boogie-woogie moves. Many famous people came over—Ray Charles, Perry Como, Johnny Cash, Brenda Lee, and Sam Phillips from Sun Records. This was a normal Friday (or Tuesday or Wednesday) night to Dad and his half-sister, Lycrecia.

Now, Sam and Katie are having a fairly normal upbringing. It cracks me up how strict Dad can be. He's got a block on TV channels, including MTV and VH1!

He is on the road a lot less than he used to be, maybe thirty or forty days a year. These days, when he has a show, he gets up at 5:00 in the morning, flies to the show, plays the concert, and flies home that same night. All told, he spends many more days hunting, fishing, or searching for Civil War relics than doing the showbiz thing. He always says, "This music business stuff interferes with my hunting and fishing something terrible."

Even though we didn't have him around like Katie and Sam do now, when we were with him, he acted like a normal dad. We would forget he was famous—except when we were out with him in public.

When we were out to dinner, someone almost always came up and asked for his autograph. And even when people didn't come up to us—in Nashville, people see a lot of stars and usually try to leave them alone—we could tell that they recognized him. We'd see the looks on their faces and notice them trying not to look. But sometimes, people couldn't hide their reactions.

Like the day Dad picked me up to take me to TCBY in Green Hills, the part of Nashville where we lived. He must have been on his way to a show because he was wearing his stage clothes. Well, we were standing in line, and I was squinting to see the menu, trying to decide whether to get sprinkles on my frozen yogurt, when this man turns around, sees Dad, and passes out cold. He fell face-down on the floor. After a minute or two, he was sitting up, so Dad leaned down, smiled at him, and said, "You okay, son?"

The poor guy couldn't speak. I wasn't sure what to do, but Dad was used to this kind of thing, so we just politely stepped past the man and placed our order. Then we went on our way.

Holly says the first time she realized that Dad was different than other dads was when she brought him to school for a father-daughter breakfast when she was in the third grade. She and Dad were sitting at a table, and everyone—the teachers, the kids, even all the other dads—lined up to get his autograph. It was a huge, long line that wrapped all the way around the cafeteria and out the door. The breakfast buffet was just sitting there empty, with no one in line. The food was getting cold while everyone stood there waiting for Dad.

Of course, Dad didn't always have to be there for Holly and me to be reminded he wasn't an ordinary father. Like Holly, I also had a stand-out experience when I was in the third grade. That year, Dad was named the Country Music Association's Entertainer of the Year, yet again. The morning after the big award show, my teacher made me get up in front of the class and read aloud a newspaper story about the award. I was really glad Dad won, but I was also incredibly shy. I hated speaking in front of people, so I was mortified.

I wanted to crawl into a hole and hide every time a boy at school called me "Hank" or "Bocephus." But that kind of stuff would usually die down a few weeks after the big award shows.

But for die-hard fans, things never died down. Sometimes, they would come looking for Hank Jr. Once, Holly and I were staying over at his house. When I woke up in the morning, I walked downstairs, opened the curtains, and came face to face with a man holding a video camera. I was too startled to scream. Dad had long been used to this stuff. People have been photographing him since he was a little boy walking out of his house to get on the school bus on Franklin Road in Nashville. He just opened the front door and calmly but firmly told the guy with the video camera that he'd have to leave.

Another time, when I was around ten years old, I was staying with my stepmom at Dad's house in Paris, which didn't have a gate. People could drive right up to the house, and one night these people came roaring up the driveway, completely drunk. They were screaming and revving the car engine and one guy was firing off a gun! Dad wasn't home and we were freaking out but when nobody came outside the people in the car finally just drove off.

Usually, if fans came by, they would just drive up, take a picture, then turn around and leave. Or, sometimes they'd get out and knock on the door: "Is Hank here?"

Usually, we'd tell them they had the wrong house—"Sorry, he doesn't live here . . . "—and that would take care of it.

I've never been embarrassed to be my father's daughter. But as a kid, especially a shy kid, it was sometimes challenging for me to have a famous father. For example, there was the time I went to camp and the kids found out who my dad was and they kept snapping pictures of me during the bus ride out to the campsite. I wasn't embarrassed of him; I was just self-conscious.

Now that I'm older, it's much easier to handle. And if people don't know who my Dad is, I sometimes choose to keep it that way. Holly, too.

Not long ago, Holly was in Wal-Mart somewhere in Georgia, and the guy standing in the line in front of her was wearing a Bocephus T-shirt. At one point (I think the clerk was moving slowly), he turned around and smiled at her. She smiled back without making mention of the shirt.

Some things are just better left unsaid.

Chapter 8

Family Secrets

Even though I never met my grandfather Hank Williams, I see him or hear from him pretty much every day.

I'll drive down Broadway and see him grinning back at me from a billboard or I'll see his silhouette on a smattering of Hatch Show Print posters plastered across an empty store front. Or I'll turn on the radio and hear Norah Jones singing "Cold, Cold Heart" or Patty Griffin singing "House of Gold" some sixty years after he wrote those songs. I'll turn on the TV and there's Dave Matthews and Neil Young singing "Alone and Forsaken" at the Hope for Haiti Now concert. Or my friend Kellie Pickler tells me that the first song she ever learned was "My Bucket's Got a Hole in It." You just can't escape the guy.

Every time he shows up, I try to think of him as a guardian angel. So if I'm out to dinner in Nashville and open a menu where the entrées consist of Long, Gone Lonesome Blue Corn Chowder or Hey, Good Lookin' Linguine, I don't get annoyed by the tackiness or commercialization of it all. I usually don't even say anything out loud. Instead, I give him a silent wink and a nod and I smile to myself, as if he and I were sharing a secret.

I think it's cool that there are reminders of my grandfather and grandmother all over Nashville. I always think of them when I drive past certain places, especially their old house at 4916 Franklin Road.

Back when they bought the house in 1949, that part of Franklin Road was surrounded by farmland and considered to be way out in the country, even though it was only a few miles from downtown. As soon as they moved into what was originally a three-bedroom brick house, Audrey immediately began adding on rooms and making plenty of decorative changes, including a one-of-a-kind wrought iron railing adorned with the notes from the first few bars of "Lovesick Blues." I wonder if this is where Elvis got the idea for the gates at Graceland.

The interior was either glamorous or tacky, depending on your point of view. I would have loved to have seen the Asian artwork and rugs and my grandmother's heart-shaped bathtub and headboard in her bedroom.

Although Audrey lived in the house until she died there in 1975, at one point during the 1980s, a large section of the home was actually moved to Music Row and turned into a museum, where my Aunt Lycrecia, Dad's half-sister, led the tours. Since then, the house has changed hands several times. In 1992 Tammy Wynette bought the house and lived there until her death in 1998. Today, the property is owned by the church next door.

Even though the house looks completely different than it did when Hank, Audrey, Lycrecia, and Dad lived there, I would love to go inside, but I've never gotten the chance. I got close one time, though, when I was in grade school and my Girl Scout troop leader hosted a sleepover for thirty girls at her home, which was right next door. The sleepover was one of those wild slumber parties where the girls stay up all night and pull pranks, such as stealing each other's bras and underwear, filling them with water, and sticking them in the freezer. Between all our squealing and laughing, I remember looking out the window at one point and imagining all the scenes that played out in the house where Dad grew up. I know they'd been knocked down and rearranged and added to, but if those walls could only talk, I'd love to hear the stories.

My grandparents met in Banks, Alabama, back in 1943 when Hank Williams came to town as one of the performers in a traveling medicine show, a moving cabaret sponsored by the makers of various miracle cure potions, like "snake oil," that were supposed to cure diseases, get rid of wrinkles, prolong life, and so forth. Think of a black-and-white infomercial with wagons and traveling musicians. This was a long way from Bonnaroo.

At medicine shows, the performers played their songs, and then, afterward, they actually went out in the audience and hawked the products. My grandmother told a reporter that she first met my grandfather when he came up to her car after the show and asked if she'd like to buy some of the herbs they were selling, which she didn't. Instead, Hank, Audrey, and Audrey's Aunt Ethel went out to see another show later that night. On their second date, Hank asked Audrey to marry him.

Part of her thought he was crazy, but the other part of her was crazy about him. Even so, they couldn't get married right away because, technically, Audrey was still married to her first husband, Erskine Guy, who she'd eloped with just prior to her eighteenth birthday. The young couple had a baby girl, Lycrecia. Not long after that, Erskine Guy went to work one day and never came back. Audrey never heard from him again.

So a divorce was pending, and as soon as it came through, she and my grandfather were married on December 14, 1944, at a gas station near Andalusia, Alabama.

I always wondered why Hank and Audrey got married at a gas station. Were they in a hurry? Just passing through? But as it turns out, it was a practical thing. The man who owned the gas station just happened to be a justice of the peace. So they met him there and he performed the ceremony. Not exactly glamorous, but that would come later.

By all accounts, between the two of them, Audrey was the one with the ambition and the drive—kind of like Sharon Osbourne with an Alabama accent. I have heard and read dozens of times that without her, Hank Williams would have never become a star. He definitely had the talent, but he didn't always have the motivation. He liked to drink and he didn't always follow through. During their few years together, Audrey made sure that he did.

Audrey was the second strong woman in my grandfather's life. The first was Hank's mother, my great-grandmother Lillie. She was a big woman, standing almost six feet tall, and she was tough. My great-grandfather Lon worked as a logger and the family— Lon, Lillie, and their two kids, Hiram (later, "Hank") and Irene— moved around a lot, mostly in southern Alabama.

For different stretches of time, they actually lived in railroad boxcars in logging camps, as many lumber families did. At other times, they rented homes and ran different businesses, including a strawberry farm and a country store. Then, when Hank was just six years old, his father was hospitalized and spent the next ten years in a Veterans Administration hospital dealing with the effects of trauma and injuries he'd suffered during World War I. So, basically, Hank grew up without a father. His mother took on the role of head of the household, and she was more than up to the task.

Lillie worked in a cannery and as a night nurse in a hospital for a time, but mostly, she supported the family by running a boarding house. Then, years later, when my grandfather got into music and started playing shows, Lillie actually drove the band to their gigs. I love the image of my big, strong, great-grandmother behind the wheel in the front seat, while all these twenty-something and teenage guys and their guitar cases are all crammed in the back of her '37 Chevy!

At the shows, Lillie collected money at the door, making sure to take her cut off the top to reimburse herself for gas before paying the band. If necessary, she also worked as a bouncer. I guess she was good at her job because Hank once told a reporter, "There ain't nobody in the world I'd rather have alongside me in a fight than my mama with a broken beer bottle in her hand."

Lillie always supported her son's musical ambitions, encouraging him when he sang at home or in church and buying him a guitar—a huge investment during the Depression—when he was eight years old.

Young Hiram, or "Harm" as they called him back then, might have been drawn to music when he was young partly because he was a frail boy who was born with a spinal deformity, spina bifida occulta, and couldn't really play sports. He was also lonely a lot. He missed his Dad, and in the evenings, his mother basically ignored him when she was busy cleaning up after dinner at the boarding house.

However, loneliness can breed creativity. I like to think of my grandfather as a little boy, sitting outside in the dark, dreaming as he plunked away at his guitar.

Hank got serious about his guitar when, at age eleven, he befriended a black street musician named Rufus Payne, better known as Tee-Tot, who taught him everything he knew about playing the blues. Evidently, Lillie would pay Tee-Tot for lessons by making him dinner, or Hank would work delivering newspapers or selling peanuts and then go find Tee-Tot and pay him fifteen cents to show him how to pick out a few chords. After he became successful, Hank always credited Tee-Tot as his major influence, saying, "All the music training I ever had was from him."

In 1937 the family moved to Montgomery, Alabama, where Lillie started another boarding house. That same year, Hank made his first radio appearance on WSFA in Montgomery. As the story goes, he was singing and playing his Silvertone guitar in front of the radio station and the producers invited him to sing on the air. Soon, "The Singing Kid," as he was called, had his own fifteen-minute show, and it wasn't long before he became one of the station's most popular performers. The audience's response to his music encouraged Hank, and even though he was only sixteen, he quit school that year to pursue music full time.

Between his radio shows, Hank and his band, The Drifting Cowboys, played concerts in beer joints and school houses—anywhere that would have them. Some of these early gigs weren't amplified, so Hank really had to struggle to be heard, which helped him develop a strong voice as well as a thick skin.

Lillie often served as the band's road manager during the next couple of years. As far as her personal life goes, in 1939 she divorced Lon and remarried Indian Joe Hatcher, Hank's guitar player. When Hatcher died of appendicitis just a few months later, Lillie married a Cajun serviceman named James C. Bozard, whom she later divorced. After that, Lillie married one of her boarders, Bill Stone. Mrs. Lillie Stone kept running her own business while helping Hank with his career. Sometimes, her primary role as manager was to keep her son away from alcohol—not an easy task.

Unfortunately, by this point in his life, Hank had already developed a strong drinking habit. He first picked up the bottle when he was only eleven years old, when he and his cousin J. C. McNeil used to sneak shots of whiskey down by the railroad tracks. He'd been binge drinking ever since.

Sometimes he'd be dry for weeks, but then, inevitably, his back would start hurting and he'd drink to dull the pain. Or someone would bring out beer or a bottle of whiskey and he'd start drinking again just because. More often than not, he wouldn't stop for days. Promoters and other people in the record business knew

Dad and Mom as newlyweds.

Me, Mom, and Dad on Dad's plane (1979).

Bocephus? He was always just "Dad" to me.

An early duet with Dad at our house in Alabama.

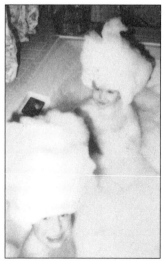

Holly and me in the tub: a prelude to our years of fashion shows.

Me at age 3 with
my ever-present
cowboy boots.

At our house in
Cullman, Alabama.
(Yes, Dad shot the bear.)

Me and Holly during a
rare snow day at our house
in Cullman, Alabama.
I have no clue why we are
wearing bathing suits.
(Note: my cowboy boots.)

If he's Big Foot (check out his cap) then I must be Little Foot.

(L to R): My grandparents, June and Warren White, with Holly, Mom, and me on vacation in Florida.

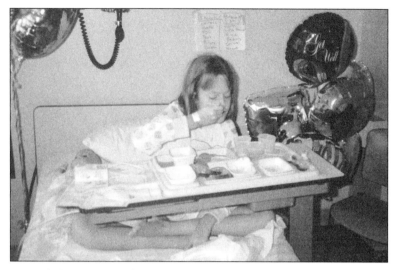

At Vanderbilt Hospital after I was diagnosed with juvenile diabetes at age 8.

Ready to cut the cake at my New Kids on the Block 12th birthday party.

Me and Holly
(ages 12 and 10),
with Shelton
(age 19).

Aunt Jo Lynn
stopped by for a hug
from me and Holly
before attending the
BMI Awards.

Holly (with brown hair!) and me on Dad's tour bus (1993).

Holly, me, and Katie (on Holly's lap) hanging out at one of Dad's shows (July 1996).

Dad and me at his house in Paris, Tennessee, before we set out on four-wheelers.

At the hospital in Memphis not long after the accident. I hate this picture but it reminds me how far I've come!

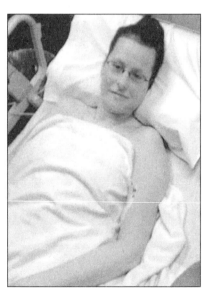

My guitar was a welcome companion during the weeks I was classified "bed to wheelchair only." (Photo courtesy of Krystal Kinnunen, krystalography.com)

Even after spending months in my hospital bed in Mom's living room, I always tried to keep a smile on my face.

A hug from my little brother, Sam, was the best medicine
while I was recuperating at home.

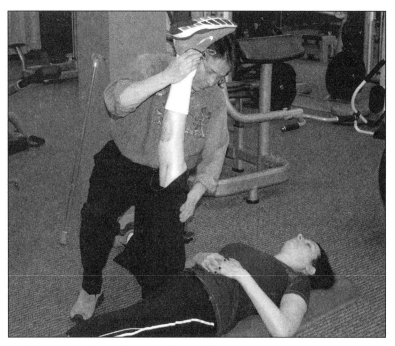

Working out with my fantastic physical therapist, Karen Pryor.

Out and about in my wheelchair: Bobby Tomberlin (left), Dolly Parton, and me at the Park Café in Nashville.

Holly, me, Dad, Sam, and Katie on the day I officially walked for the first time after the accident (September 11, 2006).

Me and Sheryl Crow at the premier party for the movie *August Rush* in Nashville (2007). I definitely just wanted to have some fun.

Ready for some sun (and more fun) after months in bed.

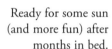

Our friend Jessica Simpson with Dad, Holly, and me before the taping of the Hank Jr. CMT Giants show in Los Angeles (2007).

Hanging out with Bobby, a.k.a. "Kid Rock."

Me and Holly with Dad when he won Icon of the Year at the BMI Awards in 2008.

Superbowl MVP Tom Brady posed for a picture with me at the 2009 Kentucky Derby.

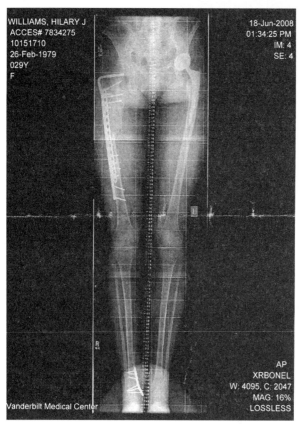

The final X-ray (a.k.a. "my bionic woman" snapshot) following surgery #23. And, yes, it is a pain going through security at the airport.

With cousin Sarah Beth at Holly's wedding in 2009. (Not pictured: the cast on my left arm.)

Me and Kellie Pickler watching *Monsters vs. Aliens* in 3-D! (2009)

Warming up backstage with Holly and Chris before Holly's show in Zurich (January 2010).

Me, Mom, and Holly in Zurich, Switzerland (January 2010).

about this and it gave Hank a reputation for being unreliable. But he was such a good performer. And he was starting to write some really good songs.

In 1941 World War II broke out, and even though Hank didn't get drafted because of his bad back, most of the guys in his band did. It was hard to find replacement players, and gas rationing was in effect so he was hardly playing any shows. So he spent the next couple of years bouncing between jobs in the shipyards in Mobile and playing shows in Montgomery and other parts of Alabama. One of those shows was the traveling medicine show in Banks, where he met Miss Audrey Mae Sheppard.

By 1944 they were married and Audrey took over Lillie's job as band manager and Hank's wrangler. Two years later, at Audrey's urging, she and Hank took the train to Nashville to meet with music publisher Fred Rose, whose company, Acuff-Rose, signed him to a songwriting deal. Around that same time, Rose brokered a deal for Hank to record four songs for Sterling Records. That led to him signing with MGM records, and in the fall of 1947 "Move It On Over" became the first big Hank Williams hit, followed by "Honky Tonkin'," which charted in 1948.

On the surface, things were going great, but those who knew him well knew that Hank was struggling. He was drinking, and that caused tension in the band, tension with Rose, and knock-down, drag-out fights with Audrey.

From the time they first got together, my grandparents fought, usually about Hank's drinking. But they fought about other things, too. They fought about money. They fought about Lillie. They fought when one of them thought the other was flirting or cheating with someone else. And frequently they fought about singing.

Audrey desperately wanted to play and sing in the band and on Hank's records. Although she played a pretty good stand up bass, she wasn't a great singer. So there was a constant tug-of-war between her, my grandfather, the band, and record producers. But mostly, it was drinking that caused their biggest problems, and in April 1948 Audrey filed for divorce.

Around the same time, Rose became so exasperated with Hank and his drinking that he wrote him a long letter basically telling him to get his act together. I'm not sure if it was the letter or the divorce papers or the combination of the two, but something clicked. Hank got it together, and although the divorce was granted in May, he reconciled with Audrey; the divorce was declared null and void one year later.

My grandfather desperately wanted to be invited to join the Grand Ole Opry, but no invitation came, probably due to the stories about his drinking. But in August 1948 he did the next best thing when he joined the lineup of a new radio show, the *Louisiana Hayride*, and became a major part of their Saturday Night Jamboree.

A funny thing happened during some of these shows. He began playing an old cover tune, "Lovesick Blues," and the crowd loved it, especially when he wobbled his knees during the song's yodel. The crowd's response prompted him to record "Lovesick Blues" the next time he was in the studio. Fred Rose hated the song and the guys in the band agreed and tried to talk Hank out of recording it. But Hank insisted, so they laid down a track of it at the end of a session, playing the song all the way through just two times. Then, in February 1949 "Lovesick Blues" became a smash. It went to number one and stayed there for sixteen weeks. It was huge. After that, Hank Williams was a major star.

In May 1949 Randall Hank Williams, also known as Hank Jr., was born. My grandfather nicknamed him "Bocephus" after Opry comedian Rod Brasfield's ventriloquist's dummy. Then— speaking of the Opry—one month after Dad came along, Hank Sr. made his famous Grand Ole Opry debut where, as legend has it, the audience at the Ryman Auditorium called him out for six encores. Just after his triumphant Opry appearance, Hank and Audrey moved to Nashville, with baby Hank and seven-year-old Lycrecia in tow.

Stardom gave my grandfather a lot of choices and creative freedom, and despite the fact that his biggest hit was a cover song, he went on to play and record mostly his own music—and hit big with it—for the rest of his career.

Freedom also allowed him to experiment and occasionally slip into the very noncommercial alter ego of Luke the Drifter to record a series of narrations and talking blues. He knew these "songs" would be a hard sell, but they were important to him, so he put them out anyway.

Many times I have heard people talk about the appeal of Hank Williams's music. To me, his songs are simple, approachable, and relatable. That's why so many artists, from Patsy Cline and Willie Nelson to Tony Bennett and Little Richard, have covered his songs over the years. And it wasn't just what he wrote, but how he wrote. I love how people describe how my grandfather wrote songs during those years when he was on the road all the time. He'd often write on scraps of paper or the closest thing he could find, even if it was the cardboard stiffener from inside a new shirt. He'd use whatever light was available, even if that meant the tiny light that came on when he opened the glove compartment in the moving car. Evidently, he also wrote songs really fast. He once said, "If a song takes longer than thirty minutes or an hour [to write], I throw it away."

I could never write a song that fast. Then again, I haven't had all the inspiration he had in his life. I know a little bit about pain, but he was racked with physical pain from the time he was a little boy. And I can't begin to touch the emotional pain that inspired so many of his songs. His songs sounded real because they were real.

It seems as though every time he was on the rocks with Audrey, he wrote a hit song. As the story goes, he wrote "Cold, Cold Heart" after he found out that Audrey had an abortion without telling him. He only found out about it when she was hospitalized with a bad infection after the procedure. And it's easy to imagine what provided the inspiration for "Long Gone Lonesome Blues" and "Your Cheatin' Heart." It doesn't take a genius to figure out what motivated "Mind Your Own Business" or "You're Gonna Change (or I'm Gonna Leave)."

Great songs.

Despite the legacy of these songs, Hank and Audrey didn't always fight. They loved each other passionately and they had a lot of happy times together during the years my grandfather was so successful. It makes me sad that those happy times often got derailed.

Over and over, Hank tried to quit drinking, making sporadic visits to sanitariums, which were nothing like the rehab or addiction centers of today. Really, they were just places where patients couldn't get a hold of liquor. In other words, he'd go there to dry out. Then, when he went on the road, it would start all over again. It was a vicious cycle of pain, drinking, pain, and drinking, with short bursts of happiness and triumph in between.

Unfortunately, pain informed my grandfather's life. Even as his career took off, his spinal condition continued to deteriorate. Then, in the fall of 1951 he fell during a hunting trip, and the pain in his back escalated to the point at which he could barely walk. He did not want to have surgery, but he knew he had no choice.

So on December 13 of that year, he checked into Vanderbilt Hospital for a procedure to repair ruptured discs and shattered vertebrae in his spine. Even though his doctors weren't ready to release him, Hank insisted on leaving the hospital on Christmas Eve, which may have aggravated his condition. Audrey got upset with him for disobeying the doctors, so he threw a chair at her. He ended up back in the hospital.

A few days later, he came home to the house on Franklin Road to recuperate. The operation hadn't gone well, and he was still in excruciating pain. He was also angry at Audrey, who he accused of being unfaithful. Then, according to interviews that were published years later, on December 29, Audrey said Hank was drinking and attacked her during an argument, so she took the kids to stay with friends. The next day, she returned to pack some clothes for a trip. (In fact, she was heading to Baltimore to apologize to the audience personally because Hank was forced to miss a New Year's Eve show due to the operation.) While she was leaving the house, she heard four gun shots. She wasn't sure if he was aiming at her or if he wanted her to think he had shot himself. In any case, she didn't stick around to find out.

Audrey went to Baltimore. Then she asked him to move out.

In January my grandfather moved out and my grandmother filed for divorce—this time for keeps.

The year that followed was the most tumultuous year of Hank Williams's life. It would also turn out to be the last year of his life, and no writer of hillbilly songs or great novels could spin a more outrageous tale.

After moving out of the family house, Hank went to stay at a hotel, then at his mother's boarding house. Then he came back to Nashville and moved across town to share a house with Ray Price. Later that year, he moved back to Shreveport to rejoin the *Louisiana Hayride* after he'd been fired from the Opry.

The entire year was a blur of missed shows, bad shows, good shows, drinking, and self-medicating with ever-stronger prescription painkillers, including morphine and chloral hydrate, a dangerous sedative and anti-anxiety drug that he got from a fake doctor, H. R. Toby Marshall. This bogus MD was treating Hank's pain while also giving him strong sedatives and painkillers to "treat" his alcoholism, which was a bizarre approach that some people actually subscribed to back then. Unfortunately, he convinced my grandfather that he could help him and was even put on the payroll for $300 a week.

Marshall was more than a phony. He was a crook. He'd been arrested for armed robbery and forging a check. The prescription pads he used were stolen. Although he was later arrested and served time for prescribing medication that contributed to the death of Hank Williams and even Marshall's own wife, it was too little, too late.

No matter how he was getting it, however, the bottom line was that Hank was getting multiple prescriptions for really strong drugs and taking way too much of them. In several books, including Colin Escott's biography, Hank is quoted as saying, "It says, take one every four hours. Maybe I ought to take four every hour, that's four times as good, isn't it?"

The only problem is that if you take four instead of one, your tolerance becomes really high. This actually happened to me in the hospital. If your tolerance becomes too high, then the medication doesn't work as well. You need more pills to relieve the pain, and sometimes your body can't handle it. The risk of an overdose is huge.

I think one misconception that people have is that my grandfather was taking pills to get high. I really don't think that's the case. I think he was numbing pain just so he could get through the day.

I know from experience that after you've been taking morphine or other powerful painkillers for a while, your body starts to crave them. If you don't ease off of them, your body gets to a point at which it needs the drugs just to function. I remember going through major DTs when I was coming off Oxycodone in the hospital. I sweated and shook and got physically sick until the drug was out of my system. I was relieved to be done with it.

So Hank was deteriorating physically. Besides sleep deprivation caused by the constant travel of the last few years and the stress of career pressure, his romantic life was a mess. The divorce was a bitter one. Then, in October he married Billie Jean Jones, a gorgeous nineteen year old he'd met in Nashville in June when she came to a show with Faron Young.

Hank actually married Billie Jean three times: once for a justice of the peace in Minden, Louisiana, and twice more at the New Orleans Municipal Auditorium for a combined audience of over 28,000 paying guests.

When he and Billie Jean were taking their vows, a former girlfriend, Bobbie Jett, was already pregnant with his child. Billie Jean knew about this and was in the loop when, the week before the wedding, Hank signed a paper saying he would pay for the birth and accept responsibility for the child. Bobbie would receive money for expenses and a one-way ticket to Southern California, where she'd lived before, and Hank's mother, Lillie, would adopt and care for the baby.

Two months later, Hank Williams was due to play a show in Canton, Ohio, on New Year's Day, 1953. He was also due to play a New Year's Eve show the day before in Charleston, West Virginia. He hired a college student, Charles Carr, to drive him from Montgomery to Knoxville, where he planned to catch a plane to Charleston. Early on December 31, he boarded the plane, but it was turned back due to fog, so he and Carr checked into the Andrew Johnson Hotel in Knoxville for a couple of hours.

Around 11:00 p.m., Carr and a couple of porters carried my inebriated grandfather to the car and put him in the backseat of his 1952 Cadillac. Carr began driving northeast. Then, somewhere between Mt. Hope and Oak Hill, West Virginia, he looked into the backseat and noticed that the blanket Hank had been sleeping under had slipped off his long, thin body. When Carr reached back and touched him, he found him cold. Hank Williams was dead.

The official cause of death was heart failure.

Sometimes people forget how young my grandfather was when he died; he was only twenty-nine years old. I think of him, marrying my grandmother when he was just twenty-one and having his first huge hit song when he was just twenty-four. That sounds so young to me! He packed all these experiences into a condensed and meaningful life—a life that inspired people both then and now.

A few days after he died, a memorial service was held in Montgomery, and even though the Municipal Auditorium, where the service was held, only had room for three thousand people, some twenty thousand fans lined the street and waited to file past his open casket.

There's a very sad story about his father, Lon, who went to a florist to buy some flowers before attending the funeral. He told the florist that he was a poor man and only had $5 to spend, and they made him a beautiful bouquet regardless.

My grandmother Audrey, who told people that right before he died, she and Hank had made plans to reconcile, was completely devastated. My dad was only three years old when his father died, so he doesn't remember much about him or the time after he died. But Audrey's daughter, Lycrecia, says Audrey never got over it.

One of the most heart-wrenching things I have ever heard is that Audrey used to write him letters long after he died and stash them in her dresser drawer. She often blamed herself for his death, and sadly, she turned this pain back onto herself when, over the years, she began abusing alcohol and became addicted to painkillers.

Unfortunately, when he died, my grandfather didn't just leave left behind the people who loved him; he also left behind a seriously tangled web of legal issues that would take years to sort out. In fact, they are still being sorted out.

Five days after he died, Bobbie Jett's baby was born. As agreed, Lillie did adopt the baby, Antha Belle Jett, who she renamed Cathy Yvonne Stone, but when Lillie died two years later (on my birthday, February 26), Cathy became a ward of the state of Alabama. Then, in 1956 she was adopted and raised by Wayne and Louise Deupree. When Cathy turned twenty-one, because she was due to receive $2,200 from Lillie Stone's estate, her parents, knowing she would wonder why this particular woman left her money, told her about the possibility that she was the daughter of Hank Williams.

Years of legal wrangling followed as Cathy, who later changed her name to Jett Williams, fought for a share of my grandfather's estate. She finally won her lawsuit, and ever since the late '80s, has been singing professionally, mostly performing my grandfather's songs.

Jett seems like a very nice person. I've met her a few times, the first occasion being when she invited me and Holly to lunch at the Palm in Nashville. We talked for a long time, and Jett gave each of us a copy of her book, *Ain't Nothin' as Sweet as My Baby*. Holly and I have gone to a couple of parties at her house, and Jett even invited me to sing at a fundraiser a few years ago, but I was still recovering from the accident, so I had to decline.

I don't begrudge Jett wanting to know and celebrate who her father is. Even though her adoptive parents were well off and very good to her, she's had a rough life in many ways—living in foster care when she was young and all the legal hassles. I guess the only problem I have with the situation, besides the fact that it caused my Dad tons of grief, is that Jett never took a blood test. I'm sure she was advised by her lawyer, now her husband, not to do that. They let the case stand or fall based on the paper my grandfather signed, which doesn't prove Jett is his daughter. And she may well be. I'm just saying that it only proves that my grandfather took financial responsibility for raising her.

Anyway, it's done now, and I wish her well.

Because my grandfather left no will behind when he died, there was also a fight over his estate. One of my grandmother's concerns was that she—and not Billie Jean—would be entitled to perform under the name Mrs. Hank Williams.

As she argued, Hank and Billie Jean had been married for less than three months when he died. Audrey was the "real" Mrs. Hank Williams and the mother of his only son. So in August 1953 Billie Jean received a lump sum payment and signed an agreement in which she relinquished all rights to Hank's estate and to any future income from it. She also agreed not to perform as Mrs. Hank Williams.

So Audrey got to keep her title. It became a nonissue, though, because in October of that year, Billie Jean married another country singer, Johnny Horton.

The legal battles never seemed to end, though. In 1974 my grandfather's copyrights came up for renewal. By then everyone knew how valuable they were, including Billie Jean, whose husband, Johnny Horton had died long before. In October 1975 she was granted half the renewals, which was a real blow to my grandmother. (Billie Jean later sold her share to Acuff-Rose for an undisclosed amount.)

Sadly, Audrey died in November of that year. She was only fifty-two years old. She had major financial and health problems at the end of her life, and she was worried about my Dad, who had just been through his terrible accident when he fell off the mountain in Montana. But the saddest thing to me is that Audrey died with a broken heart. Things weren't all bad, though. There were a lot of good times in her life, and lately, I have learned so much about her, things I never knew before.

She was a fantastic businesswoman—way ahead of her time. She had a booking agency and a publishing company and she launched my dad's career, putting him on tour and managing him when he was young. She threw legendary parties at the house on Franklin Road. What I wouldn't give to have gotten the chance to hang out with her in the living room and have her introduce me to Jerry Lee Lewis or Ray Charles or any of her famous guests.

When I think about my grandmother, I prefer to picture her in her heyday. My voice teacher told me she once went to her house way back when to pitch her some songs, and Audrey opened the door smiling and wearing the most beautiful white leather suit she'd ever seen. That's the image I try to carry around with me.

When I think of my grandfather now, I think about the day I went with Dad to visit his gravesite in Montgomery, Alabama, a few years ago. It was a cloudy, gloomy day, but I took a few pictures anyway. When I got the pictures back, there was a light shining down from the sky to the grave. I didn't see the light when we were standing there.

But just because you can't see something doesn't mean it isn't there.

Chapter 9

Coming Home

As Mom sat in the hospital waiting for me to wake up after yet another surgery, her worries had shifted from, "Will she live?" to "What kind of life will she lead?"

Would I be in a wheelchair for months, years, or even indefinitely? If I walked, would I always need to use a walker, crutches, or a cane? Would I be able to work or drive? Would I be able to have kids? Would I be going in and out of the hospital for the rest of my life? As always, she prayed and prayed. She knew that many tough times lay ahead, although at that point, she couldn't imagine exactly what they would entail.

She confided her concerns to Dr. Kregor's nurse, Traci Delk, who did her best to encourage her. "It's not a matter of whether or not she will walk, Becky," Traci said. "It's a matter of how well she will walk. She's doing everything we ask her to do, and if she keeps doing that . . . "

During my first surgery at Vanderbilt, Dr. Kregor accomplished a lot of things. In addition to removing the internal fixator on my leg, he also checked the damage to both my hips, elevated the skin flap above my ankle, and did some other surgical chores, including internal fixation of my right calf bone and right shin bone. He also worked on my left shin bone fracture. All in a day's work.

Two days later, it was Easter Sunday, and my whole family came over after going to church.

I missed being able to go to church. I tried to compensate by watching Joel Osteen on TV or listening to preachers on the internet. But I especially missed being in church on Easter, and I would have given anything that day to go back in time and be in Louisiana at my grandparents' house for one of our huge Easter Egg hunts. It was always such a big production. We'd be all dressed up in our Sunday dresses and our little hats, and Papaw would hide eggs all over the sprawling front and backyards. He and Granny would invite all the cousins plus people from the town to come over and try to find the eggs. It was a hoot!

The few times we didn't go to Louisiana for Easter when we were younger, Holly and I visited Dad at his house in Paris, and he would hide eggs for us. There was always one very special egg, which he called "The Golden Egg." It was just one of those little neon-colored plastic eggs that twisted apart, but this particular egg had $50 inside. I think he did that for us twice, and I found the Golden Egg both times. Holly was so mad.

Whenever I knew my family or a lot of people were coming over to the hospital, I really didn't want to look sweaty or stinky. I'd always try to spruce up a little bit. This was kind of a challenge. I mean, I could put on a little lip gloss, but that was about it. I didn't have my regular face wash with me, and because I couldn't get up and go to the sink, the nurses would just kind of wipe my face with water and a wash cloth after they brought me a bowl and a cup of water so I could brush my teeth. Sometimes, though, the nurses would wash my hair, and even though it was a little bit cold and kind of drippy, it always felt amazing.

One time, while Chris Coleman (now Holly's husband) was visiting, the nurse said she was busy and asked if he would mind washing my hair. I was embarrassed that she asked him, but he said, "I don't mind at all," and took the hair-washing tray that the nurse handed him, filled it with warm water, and gently placed it under my head and neck. He cupped his hands together and scooped water onto my hair to get it wet. Then he squeezed some shampoo into the palm of one hand and using his other hand, rubbed it into a lather and smoothed it all over my head. He scooped more water onto my hair a little bit at a time and rinsed out all the suds.

When someone was this nice to me, I couldn't even speak. It was all I could do to stop myself from crying.

After the first surgery at Vanderbilt, Dr. Kregor had more information about the extent of my injuries. He had literally opened me up and had a look around, and now, he—and we—had some difficult decisions to make.

It was clear to everyone that, despite the best efforts of surgeons in Memphis, my left hip was going to fail. The arteries that sent blood into the hip had been severed and the bones had been virtually pulverized. There was little if anything left to rebuild. In cases like this, the next logical step is a total hip replacement. But because hip replacements normally don't last more than fifteen years or so, doctors don't like to perform them on young people. Dr. Kregor consulted colleagues around the country and, after much discussion, he recommended that we try to save the hip by realigning the fracture and putting in a metal plate. He told me and my parents that there was only a fifty-fifty chance of this working, but he thought the benefits outweighed the risks.

I remember feeling really confused. Then Dad, who had a lot of experience making decisions about surgical procedures, convinced me to go for it. "We've got to trust the doctors, honey," he said.

So we gave the go-ahead, and a few days after Easter, Dr. Kregor performed a seven-hour surgery to remove the old hardware in my left femur and put in a plate that he hoped would permanently mesh with the bone.

After that operation, for the time being, there was nothing more for the doctors to do. My right femur had to be fixed at some point, but as Dr. Kregor said, people can only process so much at one time. He'd addressed the left hip and the right ankle, which were the most crucial. Then, after several weeks, we would decide what to do next.

That's the way it works. It's a process. If you could get it all done in a day, you would. But there's a whole lot of waiting and seeing and adapting to be done when a bunch of really smart people are putting your body back together. After some discussion of checking me into Stallworth Rehab Center, I was relieved when the doctors said I could do my waiting and seeing at home.

Of course, I couldn't live by myself at this point, so I'd be coming home to Mom's house. At that point, neither she nor I knew how long this would be. Doctor Kregor said I'd be "non-weight bearing" and "bed-to-wheelchair only" for about three months. After that, there would be other surgeries and other stretches of "bed-to-wheelchair only." But I couldn't think about that, and neither could Mom.

For now, I was coming home.

I was happy, but I was also apprehensive. It's not as if I was changing out of my hospital gown, throwing on my street clothes, and hopping back into my regular life. In fact, I didn't even change out of my hospital gown the day I went home. I was still hooked up to monitors and an IV, so I didn't feel like attempting it.

I worried about what things would be like at Mom's house. I mean, I was bedridden. For the past six weeks, full-time, experienced nurses had been doing all the difficult work of taking care of me. They did their tasks in a hospital setting. Now, besides visits from a traveling nurse a couple times a week, Mom would be my primary caregiver. We could have hired a full-time nurse, but I didn't want that and neither did she. Incredibly, she was willing to do this. She kept saying it was her honor to take care of me.

True, she'd given me insulin shots for years, so she wasn't completely unfamiliar with nursing duties. Still, I couldn't help but feel a little nervous. I knew Holly would be around to help, too. But she still had a cast on her arm, and Mom is a tiny person. Would they be able to lift me if they had to? Were we up to this?

As soon as she got the word that I was going to be released, Mom ran around preparing for me to come live at her house. A coordinator at Vanderbilt helped her with details such as arranging for follow-up nursing care and telling her where to get a wheelchair, a walker, a shower chair, a hospital bed, and all the other things we would need. Next, a guy who works for Dad helped Mom research companies that install temporary wheelchair ramps. For logistical reasons, the ramp would need to extend from the kitchen door all the way out into the garage, so Mom and Holly got busy making space for the new contraption. The garage was full. Mom hasn't parked her car in there for years, mostly because of Holly's and my stuff. So Mom and Holly spent an entire day cleaning, throwing things out, and packing up bags for Goodwill so there would be room to move in the ramp and, eventually, wheel me in and out of the house.

On April 26, exactly six weeks after the wreck in Mississippi, a couple of orderlies came into my room, lifted me from my bed, put me on a stretcher, and then wheeled me down the hall and out the door, where they lifted me into a waiting ambulance. They locked the stretcher into place and—this was now a familiar feeling—Mom climbed in behind me for the ten-minute ride to her house.

Sign of Life

When we got there, the guys lifted the stretcher out of the ambulance and carried it to the front door. Because the ramp hadn't been installed yet, they couldn't roll me inside; they had to carry me up the steps. I remember feeling awkward and vulnerable, thinking, "Please don't drop me." But the guys were so sweet. One of them said, "Well, you're easy to carry. You must not weigh over a hundred pounds."

I had lost a ton of weight, but I didn't expect to hear something like that.

As careful as they were, it still was a bit of a bumpy ride across the yard, up the front steps, and into the living room where Mom had set up the bed. I breathed a loud sigh of relief when they set the stretcher down and lifted me up and into bed. Once I was situated, they picked up the stretcher and headed back to the ambulance. Mom walked them to the door and stood there watching as they pulled away.

Inside, the house was clean and bright and filled with balloons and flowers, most of them sent by Dad. He said he wanted the house to look like a party, and it definitely did. The truth was, though, I wasn't ready for a party. That's why only Holly came over that afternoon. That was enough for me for the time being—just me, Mom, and Holly.

I don't really remember much about that first day home. Basically, I just spent the rest of the day resting and taking in my new surroundings. I'd spent years of my life in this room, the living room of our house that was now my room because I was unable to climb the stairs to one of the upstairs bedrooms.

Mom and my Aunt Donna had moved furniture around so people could sit near me when they came to visit. The bed was next to the big window so I could see outside, and I could also see into the kitchen and talk to Mom if she was in there cooking or checking e-mail on her computer.

The far side of the living room is separated from the front part of the house by a pair of glass French doors, and even though the glass made the room nice and bright, I did feel kind of exposed because people standing at the front door could see all the way inside. Also, it was a little creepy at night, sleeping down there by myself in this big room. So my Aunt Donna decided to put up curtains over the doors. "This will give you some privacy," she said, as she pinned the curtains into place.

Aunt Donna reminds me of Paula Deen. She looks and sounds a little bit like her, plus she's an amazing cook and she can sew anything. When we were kids, she used to make pillows and bedspreads and sew matching outfits for me, Holly, and my cousin Sarah Beth. I remember these cotton sleep shirts she made for us one summer; they had big, eyelet-ruffled sleeves and our names on the front.

So when Aunt Donna came to visit and we were talking about the doors, she got up, drove over to Dillard's at the Green Hills Mall, bought two cream-colored sheets, and made curtains out of them. Then she went to Target and bought a couple of tie backs and the job was done. They looked so good that, years later, Mom still has them hanging in her house.

I guess pretty sheets were a recurring theme in the house. I always loved having brightly colored sheets on my home or hospital bed. It really lifted my spirits.

There were other additions to the living room, including a big triangle-shaped contraption hanging by its chain over the bed. This is what I used to lift myself up and, eventually, out of bed. There was a bedpan and a bucket (I got sick a lot) and a plastic hair-washing tray, which fits against your neck and has an open end for the water to roll off and away from the bed.

There was also a Porta-Potty, a little chair/toilet that I would move onto by sliding down a piece of plywood that Mom or

Holly would lean at an angle between the bed and the edge of the chair. They would pick up my legs and help me onto the board, which I literally slid down. To make the board more slippery, Mom covered it with the leg from a pair of cut-up pantyhose, which was a hint, along with putting baby powder on the bedpan, that she picked up from the nurses at the hospital. When I was done, I'd use my arms to push myself back up and either Mom or Holly would pick up my legs and get me back into bed.

A day or two after I got home, Dad came over to visit. When he walked in, he was all smiles, "Well! Look at you!" He walked over to the bed to give me a hug and I noticed that he hesitated just a little before he put his arms around me. His signature bear hug was a little softer than normal this time, which I thought was really sweet.

After a while, he turned serious and called Holly and Mom into the room. "C'mon, girls," he said. "I want us to pray."

So right next to my bed, Dad got on his knees. He motioned to Holly and Mom to join him, so they knelt down next to him and each held one of his hands. They all three put their heads down, and Dad prayed out loud, "Lord, we know she's so strong. We know Hilary is going to walk again. We know she's going to come out better than ever on the other side . . . "

Then we all sat quietly for a while and did our best to believe.

Another day he was visiting me, I remember Dad saying, "Honey, you have got to gain some weight!"

When I think about that now, it really makes me laugh. It's not like I was dieting! The whole time I was in the hospital, everything seemed to make me sick; the doctors even had to remove the epidural they put in during surgery. When one medication made me sick, they'd counterbalance it with nausea medication, usually Zofran, which helped, but rarely improved my appetite.

Even at home, I was so nauseous from all the painkillers and other medications that it was difficult to eat, or if I did manage to push down something bland like toast or a plain baked potato, I would often get sick to my stomach.

Come to think of it, I probably vomited every day for three or four months.

Poor Mom! And poor Holly! Here she was, still with a cast on her arm, and it was often her job to empty the bucket when I vomited. She would always try to make me feel better about it, smiling and singing as she took the bucket out of the room to dump it. She must have been dying. I kept saying, "I'm sorry. I'm so sorry . . . "

I remember Holly walking across the room, one arm in a sling, the other carrying a bedpan to empty out in the bathroom. Talk about drawing the short straw! The day of the accident, Holly was only two days away from leaving to play some concert dates in Germany. Mom had planned to go with her. But, of course, everything got canceled.

Every time Holly came over, she brought me something, whether it was some kind of take-out food I liked or a present, such as a gold Kate Spade iPod holder or a Tempurpedic pillow from Brookstone or these stretchy, flowing black pants that were perfect to wear to doctor's appointments.

I didn't wear jeans until many, many months after the accident because, for one thing, you can't wear pants with metal zippers when you're getting X-rays. Besides, they would have been way too hard to put on. As it was, even those black pants with the elastic waist were a struggle. I had to lie on one side, hike the pants up one leg, then flip to the other side and hike the other leg up, then inch the pants under my backside until they were all the way up under my waist. It would have been fun to try on my jeans, though, because they would have fallen right off of me. When my friends came to visit during those first few weeks, they would often say, "Oh my God, Hilary! You are so skinny!" I would say, "Yeah, I finally got the supermodel bod I always wanted."

I would have been really happy being that thin, well, maybe almost that thin, if I'd had some muscle tone. But as I lay there most of the summer looking at my skinny, flabby legs sticking out of my shorts, I came to the conclusion that my old body wasn't so bad. I wanted it back.

For the first month or so I was at home, three times a week a nurse came to the house for a quick visit. She would come in, check my vital signs, clean and dress my wounds, make notes on my chart, and so forth. Then she would hand Mom a bag of supplies, say, "Here ya' go!" and head out the door.

Every time she came, Mom would ask her a lot of questions and take plenty of notes because she knew that, by the end of the month, she would be doing all these things herself. Mom says that the most challenging thing for her was the wound care, specifically the cleaning and dressing of the skin flap above my ankle. Because the wound was on the back part of my leg, Mom first had to prop my leg high enough so she could see it, then, reaching up and under, she went through the steps to wash the raw wound with soap and water. Last, she applied salve and bandages while making sure everything was kept sterile.

Holly absolutely could not bring herself to help with this task, and I don't blame her. She did help with other things, though. She and Mom usually worked as a team to bathe me in bed, with one person rolling me to the side while the other laid down plastic and towels so the bed didn't get wet. They would take turns washing my hair, bringing me food, giving me medicine, and helping me on and off the toilet. But the twenty-four-hour duty fell to Mom. It was like she had a newborn baby again, except this time around, I was much harder to pick up and I could talk to her.

If I needed something in the middle of the night and she was upstairs sleeping, instead of crying like I did when I was a baby, I'd call her on my cell phone. I hated doing that, and I really tried to make late night calls my last resort. But sometimes, especially if it wasn't urgent, I'd just wait. Like the night when I couldn't sleep and one of my socks fell off. My foot was really cold and I just lay there in the dark staring at my bare foot and thinking how pitiful it was that I couldn't get out of bed, pick up my sock, and put it back on.

I tried not to obsess about being so helpless. I'd turn on the TV to distract myself, but as every insomniac knows, there are some really bad shows on at 3:00 in the morning. I'd lay there all sweaty; I was always sweating even though I had the chills. I'd try not to think about that, too. Then, a lot of the time, I would put on the Christian music channel on satellite and close my eyes and dream of how amazing it would feel not to be cold and sweaty and how great it would be to put on a pair of socks and a pair of shoes and get up and walk across the room.

After several weeks of rest, I was ready to start physical therapy at home. Vanderbilt Hospital paired me with physical therapist Karen Pryor, who is a PhD, a Reiki Master, and a medical intuitive with thirty years of experience working with and healing patients. She also has an extensive background in natural medicine, and the minute she showed up, I knew that I was in really good hands.

Karen is upbeat and enthusiastic, kind of like a more petite version of University of Tennessee basketball coach Pat Summitt. She encouraged more than she pushed, and from the moment we met, she convinced me that I could do absolutely anything I wanted to do.

Before the real work began, Karen helped with a lot of little things that made a huge difference in my life. For instance, one of the first things she noticed was that I was using a regular bedpan, a big thick one. She shook her head, "Why did they send you home with this? You need a fracture pan, which is thin and flat and much easier for someone with broken hips to use."

So we got one of those.

Then she sent Mom out to Wal-Mart to buy an egg crate mattress pad. This thing, which cost all of $15, was genius. Because I had a fractured pelvis and hips, it hurt to put weight on them while I was lying in bed. My bottom would kind of pooch upward to relieve the pressure, which put strain on my back. That in turn made it difficult to sleep. And as Karen pointed out, if you can't sleep, you can't lock in memories. You're in a mental fog all day. Plus, when you're not rested, it makes it hard for your body to heal. So Karen measured my hips and cut a hole in the egg crate mattress and placed it directly underneath me so my hips dropped down through the hole, which she nicknamed "the butt cave." With the weight off my hips and pelvis, I was so much more comfortable and I started sleeping better right away.

Karen also gave us other tips that made it so much more tolerable to be stuck in bed. And her solutions, such as wrapping Saran Wrap across the length of the bed before we did anything involving water, were easy and cheap. "I'm like a medical Mac-Gyver," she said, referencing the cheesy TV action show where the secret agent would build a rocket out of a match and a paperclip. "Sometimes, you have to improvise."

During those first few visits, Karen showed Mom how to roll me over when she was changing the bed sheets or changing my clothes. She helped my mom raise the legs on the Porta-Potty so I didn't have to stoop down so low to get on and off of it.

Then, after we got organized, the first thing Karen wanted to address was my feet. People with diabetes often have problems with their feet for several reasons. For one thing, diabetes can cause nerve damage, which may lead to the loss of feeling in the feet. If that happens and you step on a tack or even if you get a bad blister on your foot, you may not notice it for days and the wound could get badly infected. Other concerns include poor circulation, which reduces blood flow to the feet, or even calluses, which are no big deal to most people, but if people with diabetes allow calluses to build up, the calluses could turn into bad sores that, again, could cause infection.

Even though I hadn't stood upright in weeks, my feet were really callused, especially where the internal fixator had been in place, so Karen went to work getting the skin back to normal. Because I couldn't sit up and hang my legs over the side of the bed to soak my feet in a basin, Karen took warm, soapy towels and wrapped them around my feet after she'd covered the bottom half of the bed in Saran Wrap and then laid down plenty of dry towels. "You've only got one mattress," she said. "We've got to keep it dry."

Then Karen scrubbed my feet, taking care not to break any new skin underneath the calluses. It took a few visits to remove all the dead skin. Then, during every visit, she would keep them soft by rubbing my feet with lotion, which not only felt amazing but also increased circulation and got rid of the tingling I felt.

On the days Karen didn't come over, Mom rubbed my feet for me at least once a day. That was heavenly, but more importantly, all this rubbing was preparing my feet for the day when they would once again make contact with the floor. I could hardly wait for that. But first things first.

Before I walked—or crawled—I had to sit up in bed, which was a major challenge. Even though my hospital bed rose automatically, I had difficulty sitting upright, even if the bed was doing the heavy lifting for me, because doing so put too much pressure on my hips, femur, pelvis, and tailbone. Plus, I'd had a lot of internal trauma, so my midsection was still tender and I had very little strength in my back and my trunk.

Despite these obstacles, I started attempting to sit up, always working in very small stages. At first, I got very, very light-headed because I had been lying down for so long. My body had grown accustomed to being horizontal, so when I sat up, my blood pressure had to adjust to pump away from gravity. Sometimes, the blood wouldn't reach my head in time and I'd get dizzy and nauseous. Then Karen would give me a little bit of ginger ale and some crackers and ease me back down until I was ready to try again.

Those first few times, she fastened a belt around my waist and pulled on it to help lift me up. Then, when she thought I could sit up all the way, Karen called Mom into the room in case she needed help. That's what she said, but I think she mostly wanted Mom to watch me do it.

This was a big deal for me—and for us—and despite the spinning and the blurriness and the nausea, I couldn't help but grin. But then, I immediately lay back down because I thought I was going to faint. After a few minutes, Karen put the belt around me and I tried again. That was a typical afternoon.

Once I sat up, it was a great feeling of accomplishment but at first, I couldn't stay up for very long. I remember Dad coming over right after I'd "learned" to sit up again. Somebody was taking our picture—I think it was for a fan magazine. Anyway, I was sitting up and Dad handed me a guitar. I started playing something, but then I started slumping over. I couldn't stay up so I said, "Dad, can I lean on you?"

He came and sat down on the bed, with his back toward me. Then I leaned against him. We both cracked up and the photographer snapped a few photos.

I wish I had that picture.

Karen gave me exercises and other things to do in between her visits, and I swear I never cheated or skipped a single one of them. It was simple. I knew that the more I did, the faster I would get better. I was too young to be like this. I really, really wanted to be back to normal as soon as possible.

So when Karen told me that while I was watching TV, during every commercial I should move my arms and legs or, later, to try to pull my knees to my chest, I did it. I used the exercise bands she left with me in between her visits, too. Mom would hook them under my feet and I would pull on the bands and lift my legs just a little.

When Karen asked Mom to buy me a triangular pillow that looks like a giant wedge of cheese, Mom went and got it. Then, when Karen told me to elevate my legs on the pillow for several hours a day to eliminate excess fluids, I did it. When she told me to drink tons of water to eliminate the toxins from all the medication, even though I dreaded the thought of having a full bladder, I did it. When Karen told me to take cayenne pepper to avoid blood clots after surgery, I did it. I took the vitamins she recommended, and when I was having trouble keeping any food down, she gave us recipes for chicken soup and protein shakes, which I ate and drank. I listened to her and turned the lights down low and did my best to chill when she told me I needed to relax. "Your body can't be in fight-or-flight mode and healing mode at the same time," she said. "If you stress, your body will think it's being injured again. The wreck is over. Now, it's healing time."

I listened. And I believed.

Chapter 10

Normal

After I'd been home for a couple of weeks, someone asked me, "So when will you be back to normal?" I really don't think the person was trying to be mean; it just came out wrong. I'm sure it was just a variation of, "So when do you think you'll be up and at 'em again?" That question didn't tick me off nearly as much as, "So what do you do all day, anyway?"

In awkward situations, some people just don't know what to say. That's why I'm officially giving those people permission to say nothing.

I knew almost from the beginning that I would never be "normal" again. Although in Memphis, Dr. Croce presented me with a very encouraging timetable when he told me I'd be driving and probably walking with a cane by October, which was only seven months after the wreck. I believed him, but I knew that it would be a huge challenge. I also knew that things would never be the same.

How could they be? Parts of my body—my hips, my ankle, my legs—were held together by more plates and screws than they sell in Aisle Five at Home Depot. For the rest of my life, I would be highly sensitive to changes in the weather, feeling rainy days in my bones much like a person with arthritis does. I may walk, but I would never run. I may be able to do Pilates one day, but kickboxing was probably a bad idea. As Dr. Kregor told me months later, I could do anything I wanted to, but if it were him, he'd avoid skydiving. I added bungee jumping to the list. Luckily, I'd never really been a thrill-seeker, so I never had the desire to do that.

Who knew exactly what the future would bring? I would most likely walk again, probably with a cane, almost definitely with a limp, and I would most likely need to use a wheelchair to travel long distances through places such as the airport or the mall for the rest of my life.

The first couple of times I went out of the house were for doctor's appointments, and because I couldn't put any weight on either of my legs or even sit up for any length of time, I was transported to and from the house by stretcher and in an ambulance.

After a few weeks, I could sit up, so I got to go outside in a wheelchair. Even though we'd had the ramp built, taking me out of the house was still a big production and really hard on Mom and Holly or whoever else was there to help because they had to lift me in and out of the chair, both coming and going. They had to position me just right so I wouldn't be in pain, and they were always afraid they were going to hurt me or drop me. Still, as often as they could, Mom or Holly or my friend Angela would somehow manage to get me into the chair and take me for walks in the neighborhood.

I had been home for a couple of months when we got invited to a cookout that my friend Hugh's grandparents were having. I really, really wanted to go. The thing was, though, that I hadn't been in a car that wasn't an ambulance since the accident. So I was nervous about that. Plus there were some logistical problems.

I could sit up for a short time, but I really couldn't put weight on either of my legs, so getting me in and out of a passenger seat would be a real challenge. So Mom had the idea to rent a medical van, which at first we thought was brilliant. The van was big enough so I could ride in it without having to get out of the chair and there was a fold-out metal ramp to roll me in and out. Once inside, the wheelchair locked in place so I wouldn't roll around in the back when the van was moving.

As good as all this seemed, though, it was tough to get the chair inside while I was sitting in it. That chair was a lot heavier than it looked. Mom got frustrated and I felt bad. She had to strap each wheel down manually, which was a real struggle, and Harry Houdini couldn't have unlocked that chair once we got it into place.

We went to the cookout, though, and as fun as it was to see people, I started feeling really self-conscious. I know people didn't mean it, but it seemed like everybody was staring at me. Then, I got really dizzy and sick, and after only thirty minutes or so, we had to leave. But I'm not sorry we went. It was like I'd jumped over another hurdle on the way back to normal.

After we turned in the van, Mom and Holly started taking me out in Mom's Suburban (the seats in smaller cars were way too low), whenever they could.

Every time we went out, it was like planning the D-Day Invasion. First, they had to get me from the bed into the chair. Then, once they rolled me outside, they had to get me out of the chair and into the passenger seat. Then, they had to stow the chair in the back. When we got where we were going, hopefully there was an available handicapped parking space; don't get me started about people who park illegally in handicapped parking spaces. Next, they had to get the chair out of the back, set it up, then lift me out of the passenger seat and back into the chair. Then, although I got pretty good at wheeling myself, they usually had to push me around.

It was a little easier on whomever was helping me when one leg had healed enough so I could put some weight on it. Then I could step out of the chair and balance on one leg while I lowered myself backward into the passenger seat of the car. Once I was sitting down, I could pick up my legs one at a time with my hands and put them in the car. Despite these small improvements, at that point in my life, there was no such thing as a quick trip.

Still, except for the times right after a surgery, Mom or Holly or Angela would manage to take me somewhere once or twice a week just so I could get out. We went to the mall or out to eat Mexican food. Once, they even took me to McDonald's, just to get a hamburger at the drive-thru. But without a doubt, one of the best trips I took in the wheelchair was into my own front yard.

It was a really hot, sticky summer day. Anyone who's been to Nashville in June knows the kind of day I'm talking about, when your clothes and skin are drenched the moment you step or, in my case, wheel outside.

First, Mom helped me change into a bathing suit. Then she opened the kitchen door and I wheeled myself down the ramp. I was getting better at doing that part by myself, and I could actually roll down the ramp pretty fast. I stopped in the driveway and then Mom helped me transfer onto a patio chair. Then she went around the corner and got the hose and proceeded to spray me with it until I was completely drenched. It was hilarious, like one of those water fights you have when you're washing the car. Then she washed my hair, right out there in the front yard. It felt so good—like a religious experience.

Not long after that, Holly and Mom bought a kiddie pool at Target and brought it home. I tried taking a bath outside, but that didn't work very well; I really couldn't get into it and the water went all over the place. It would be over a year before I could get into a real bathtub.

You don't know how much you miss baths or showers when you haven't had one in a while. Ever since I'd gotten home, Mom had been bathing me in bed with a washcloth and I'd been dreaming of a real shower. Then, my dream came true when

Holly came home one day and said that her friend Laura Stroud invited me over to use their steam shower. It was perfect for me because it was on the first floor, so besides the small steps leading into the house, there would be no stairs to climb. Plus, the shower was a walk-in, so I wouldn't have to take a big step like you would over a bathtub, and it had a built-in seat, so I could sit down. As if that wasn't enough, the shower was gorgeous, all cream-colored marble, with different shower heads and spray settings.

It was a chore getting into the house and finally into the bathroom and the shower, but I was determined. This was too good to pass up. I used my walker going in, and then Holly and Mom lowered me down to the seat, and when I was done, they helped me back up again.

Possibly the best part of that shower was the fact that I could finally shave my legs. I had to be really careful as I tentatively navigated around my scars and stitches. But it felt amazing. I wanted to sit there and let that spray rain down on me forever.

I was so tired after my big shower outing that I did nothing else that day. I was too exhausted to do anything else. I fell right to sleep. When I woke up, everything was sore from all the moving around. Imagine, being sore from shaving your legs! But I was clean. Gloriously clean. I don't remember feeling that good before or since.

Sometime in June, I started having major pain in my left hip, around the area where the plate had been inserted. When his schedule cleared in July, Dr. Kregor was going to do another surgery, most likely to remove the plate, check for infection, then insert a new one. But then the pain got worse.

I remember being out with Angela at a Kenny Chesney concert at the stadium in Nashville. This was my first concert since the accident, and I was so glad to be there. I'd never noticed handicapped ramps in the stadium before but now I can tell you where every single one is located. At the show, everybody was so nice to me; a couple of guys even lifted me up in my wheelchair and set me down on a raised platform by the soundboards so I could see the stage.

But I could not ignore the pain. Every time I moved, it felt like someone was stabbing me; just sticking a knife right through my hip and pelvis. So the next day I called Dr. Kregor. X-rays confirmed there was "an intrusion of the adult osteotomy blade plate into the hip joint." In other words, the plate had flipped around and was jabbing into my hip.

Dr. Kregor still recommended removing the plate and inserting a new one, but at this point, I was done being a guinea pig. I know the pain was making me grouchy and impatient, but I felt like we'd given this a try and now it was time to go for a sure thing, which meant a total hip replacement.

Even though this would probably mean another surgery fifteen or twenty years down the road, I'd be in my mid-forties by then. I felt like that was a long time away and this was the best option for now. It felt like a reprieve. And who knows, maybe the technology will catapult forward in the next decade, and by the time my hip is ready to be replaced, a less painful, more lasting procedure will have been invented.

So I told Dr. Kregor to do the replacement. It took him two operations on two separate days to remove the plate, perform something called a Girdlestone procedure, then finally to complete the left total hip arthroplasty. By mid-July I was the proud owner of a new, titanium hip.

When someone asked Dr. Kregor to describe the pain a patient would feel after sustaining my injuries and enduring my surgeries, he answered with one word: indescribable.

It wasn't me asking the question. Before surgeries, I didn't want to know. And after surgeries, I had first-hand knowledge.

Dr. Kregor also said a patient described the pain of a femur fracture as worse than childbirth without any spinal blocks. I haven't had a child yet and I certainly don't plan to have one without painkillers, but this description sounds accurate.

There were two days between the hip replacement surgeries and the pain following part one was the worst I can remember ever experiencing. There was something about the process of bone being scraped and pieces of the hip taken out that caused a world of hurt.

Then, the pain following the hip replacement took center stage. I'll never forget that night. It felt like my nerve endings were on fire and that thousands of pins were pricking my leg where it had been cut. It went on for a couple of hours, and I asked for more painkillers, but the nurses said I had reached my limit and had to wait.

I was actually wailing, so I called Mom and said, "Call the 700 Club and have them pray for me." And she did. And Angela, who was working as the tour manager for Little Big Town, called and said everyone she was with on the road was praying for me, too. That seemed to help.

I don't want to cast blame on anyone at Vanderbilt. I'm sure there is a limit to the amount of painkillers a patient can be given. But that night was so bad. The next day, Dr. Kregor seemed annoyed that I'd gone through all that. Holly said that he told her if a patient is in that much agony, they might need more than "their limit." A patient in that much stress and pain could give themselves a heart attack.

Unfortunately, there was still more to learn about my pain threshold.

I had already accepted that it was important to get up and get moving after a surgery, no matter how impossible it seemed. I repeated the mantra, "Pain is a sign of life" and concentrated on complying with the therapists. But when, just a few days after my hip replacement, a PT at Vanderbilt wanted me to stand up, I thought he was completely nuts.

As Holly watched, or rather, as she sat in my room with her hands covering her face, I used the walker to push myself off the bed. Then, I shifted onto the walker. I think I could have put weight on one leg if I'd just had a hip replacement and nothing else. But I had no muscle tone on either side. My right femur was still in shambles, so there was nothing to lean on. Holly looked away as I cried out. "We've got to get you moving," the therapist said.

I sat back down and cried and cried. When I got back in bed and the pain subsided a bit, I wondered why I was hurting so bad. It seemed like this was worse than being in the ICU following the accident. But it made sense. In Memphis, I was unconscious much of the time and on so much medication that half the time, I didn't feel anything. What a gift that was.

Now, I was more aware and I had to focus on the fact that this was a good thing.

I learned the hard way that it hurts to heal.

What I remember most vividly about the period of time following the hip replacement was feeling incredibly weak. I was highly anemic, which was not unusual for me. I'd experienced anemia following every one of my surgeries due to acute blood loss during the procedures.

From the PolyHeme at the accident scene to all the units of blood I received in Memphis and while I was in and out of Vanderbilt Hospital, transfusions saved me. But how much can a body tolerate? During the two-part hip surgery, six units of blood and two units of fresh frozen plasma were pumped through my body. So maybe the anemia was my body's way of saying, enough already.

Unfortunately, this time, the anemia lasted for several weeks, even after I went back home to my bed in Mom's living room for another round of recovery. I remember a friend of Mom's coming over to visit and bring us some food. When she saw me she gasped and said, "You look just like your grandfather, Hank Senior!"

She didn't mean it as a compliment.

Like my grandfather in so many of the pictures you see of him, I was thin and pale. I was also lethargic. I was freezing, too. It was the middle of summer and I was wearing sweaters, hats, and gloves and covering myself with a big pile of blankets. I was cold and sweaty all the time.

Worst of all, I felt really, really depressed. I started having crazy thoughts, especially at night, thinking that I was going to fall asleep and never wake up. Looking back, now I know that I was just worn out from feeling bad. It's a cliché, but like most clichés, there's some truth to it: "I was sick and tired of being sick and tired."

I felt as if the pain of a sore leg or hip or ankle or tailbone or pelvis was one thing, but now I felt bad all over: My whole self. My spirit.

Then, slowly but steadily, I began feeling the smallest bit better every day. Karen began coming to the house to work with me again, and when she found out I was anemic, she brought black molasses, which tastes awful but is packed with iron. That stuff works! I took two teaspoons of that every day. "Life is in the blood!" Mom said cheerily as she loaded me up with all the blood-building foods and vitamins she could find.

Soon, my strength, such as it was, returned, and I could refocus my energy on my goal of learning to walk again.

When you think of someone taking their first steps, you picture a toddler standing up and falling over again and again until, one day, she gets her groove and takes off awkwardly and joyfully across the floor. Then, after a few steps, she falls into the proud, outstretched arms of her mother. I'm sure that was the scene when I took my first steps as a little girl. Actually, due to developmental delays, I didn't walk until I was two years old. So when I did, I know Mom was ecstatic.

All these years later, it was completely different. This time, I was a twenty-seven-year-old, six-foot-tall woman with a lot of broken bones in various stages of healing and contracting and reattaching to each other. Instead of standing up, falling down, getting up and taking off across the floor, I attempted single movements in tiny stages. Then, some days I'd find that I couldn't do the thing I did yesterday. So we'd have to start from scratch, attempting to rebuild muscle memory so my body would do what I wanted it to do, which was to walk, rather than what it wanted to do, which was to lie around.

Instead of a big breakthrough moment where all of the sudden, I took a couple of steps in a row, for me, learning to walk again involved things like putting a little bit of weight on one foot one day then a little bit more on it the next.

Even though Mom was great, always encouraging, and Dad would light up when he came over, saying, "You're doing great, honey!" the truth was that my progress was almost imperceptible to anyone but Karen and me. After I got released from the hospital, the very first steps I took were in the pool. Every week or so, I'd meet Karen at the Easter Seals facility in Nashville, which had a wheelchair lift that lowered me into the indoor heated swimming pool.

What an amazing feeling to be out of the chair and in the water. I felt like a mermaid—totally free and whole again. The water made me feel weightless. On land, I couldn't even stand, but in the pool, I could take steps and move around. The best part was, in the pool, there was hardly any pain. I would have lived in there if they'd let me.

Back at home, Karen started every session by rubbing my feet to warm up the nerve endings; after all, the bottoms of my feet barely touched the ground in months. Then she'd wrap a belt around my waist and pull me up with it. Once I was in a sitting position, I'd shift my legs to one side so they were hanging over the side of the bed. After that, I'd put my hands on the walker at my bedside for support, and when I was ready, Karen would use the belt to lift me until I was standing up behind it, using mostly my arm strength to hold myself up.

I remember that the first time I stood all the way up, Karen, who is a small, compact person, was shocked at how tall I was. "I kept pulling and you kept standing up and standing up!" she said.

Usually, I'd get so dizzy from standing that I'd have to lie back down until the spinning and the sweating stopped. My body was so used to being in a horizontal position that it took time to adjust to being vertical again. Mom or Karen would put a cold washcloth on my forehead or neck and I'd start to feel better. When the dizziness subsided, we'd try again. Eventually, I could stand for a minute or so. Then, while Karen was still holding me with the belt, I'd try to slightly lift one knee or put weight on one foot.

As slow as my progress was, I never doubted that I would walk again. But I also knew that when I did, it wouldn't look or feel the same as before. My body had changed, and as hard as the doctors tried to make my legs even, that was a near impossible task. The notes from my chart at Vanderbilt contained more exacting instructions and microscopic measurements than a manual for a space shuttle launch. Despite the doctors' best efforts, to this day, my right leg is an inch and a half shorter than my left leg. I try to remember that no one is completely symmetrical. Isn't there some urban legend about how no one has two feet that are exactly the same size? If not, I'm starting the rumor because it makes me feel less like a freak.

Throughout my therapy, my doctors communicated with Karen, sending her notes and copies of X-rays after every appointment so she would know what I was allowed to do. A big day for me was when the doctors gave permission for me to put weight on both feet. I could do it for a few seconds, but then the bottoms of my feet started to tingle; it felt like tiny needles sticking into my heels and toes. Then, pain started shooting up my right thigh, but still, I didn't want to stop. But Karen soon noticed the tears welling up in my eyes. I expected her inner-football coach to kick in, but instead, she turned soft. "Your body is talking to you," she said. "You don't have to punish yourself. Just put less weight on it."

That was just what I needed to hear.

The other thing I needed, or wanted anyway, was to go upstairs. I was dying to use the upstairs bathroom and the shower and to sleep in my old bed, and all these things were on the second floor. As soon as I was a little more stable, Karen said, "Let's do it."

First, she guided me to the bottom of the stairs using my walker. Then, while Mom went to the top of the stairs with the walker, I grabbed onto the railing with one hand and eased my way up the stairs, making my way up slowly. I held tight to the railing as I hopped up each step, leading with and putting weight on my good leg. Later, on the way down, I would lead with my bad leg. "Here's how to remember it," Karen said. "Going up, you're going to heaven. So you use your good leg. Going down, you're going to hell, so you use your bad leg." Up, heaven, good. Down, hell, bad . . .

Once I got to the top of the stairs, I put both hands on my walker and edged toward the bathroom. I had to turn the walker sideways to get in; the doorway is too narrow for it to fit in otherwise. Then, standing on one foot, I lifted the walker up so one leg was in the tub and one leg was out.

Mom helped me take off my clothes, and I held onto the walker and stepped into the shower, where I sat down in the medical shower chair Mom had just brought home. I really needed to sit down after my "step" class.

That was my first shower at home after the accident, and it made me feel like an entirely new person.

Then Mom brought the "butt cave" egg crate mattress upstairs and put in on my old bed. And that's where I slept that night. As nice as it had been to be sleeping and recuperating downstairs in the hub of the house, I was thrilled to be in my own room. I felt as if I was no longer a prisoner.

As far as getting downstairs again, I'd think about that tomorrow.

Throughout July and August I kept working with Karen several times a week and doing exercises on my own every day. By early September I had graduated from using a walker to walking on crutches. Then I walked using two canes. And finally, I walked with only one cane. The day I did that, September 11, 2006, is the day I officially count as the day I walked again.

Dad was coming over with his friend J. B. Billheimer as well as Katie and Sam to go to lunch with me, Mom, and Holly. So I got dressed, put on a pair of boots, and walked outside and down the front steps using just one cane.

Then I went to lunch with my family. It hurt like crazy, but I walked from the car to the restaurant and to our table using only my cane for support. When I say I walked, it was really more like a waddle. I still had so many broken bones and everything was so tight that I kind of swayed side to side as I took each step. When we finished lunch, I picked up my cane and walked back to the car. When we got home, I walked back up the steps and into the house.

I've never run a marathon or even a 10K race, but that day, I wished there was a finish line tape stretched out across the doorway. I would have dropped my cane for a minute, put my hands in the air, and burst right through it. But instead, I walked inside and went to lie down.

After that, my walking continued to slowly improve even though I almost always walked with a very pronounced limp. My physical therapist would say, "Squeeze your butt! Squeeze your hips! Tighten your core! It will help you walk straighter." I'd done a lot of squeezing and tightening of my muscles while lying in bed in the hospital and at home. But you don't know how hard it is to do all that while you're walking.

The other thing was that I could feel the metal in my body when I walked. Sometimes I could feel it shift, which was a little spooky. I can still feel it sometimes. And, unfortunately, I still limp, especially when I'm in pain. It's my body's way of protecting itself by making another area of the body work harder so the injured area doesn't have to.

These days, I usually walk without a cane. I almost always bring one with me, though, just in case. I feel more secure having it with me. That way, if I end up walking a really long distance or start to feel unsteady, I've got some backup.

Dad loves the fact that I carry a cane so, as he says, I can beat back the boys. We were laughing about that one day when he told me, "That thing is better than pepper spray! If anyone gets out of line, you can whack the shit out of him!"

"Yeah," I said, "But you never hit someone straight on because they can grab it away from you. You go over and around." A guy I know who has a black belt told me that.

"Right," Dad said. "Come at them from the side."

My favorite cane is made of leather and snakeskin, but I only use that one every once in a while. My everyday cane is a clear, Lucite cane, which is great because it goes with everything and it's impossible to break.

Shopping for canes is never something I thought I'd be doing, but I was really happy to learn that you don't have to settle for the plain, black, grumpy old man canes that you see at the drugstore. My Aunt Jo Lynn saw an article about cool canes and turned me onto fashionablecanes.com. They have every kind of cane you can imagine, from a replica of Dr. Gregory House's walking cane with flames from the TV show *House*, to a bull organ walking cane. I'm not going to mention what that one's made of, but the Web site says it's "often mistaken for old fashioned mahogany."

At first, it was awkward trying to figure out where to stow my cane when I went places. If I leaned it against the table in a restaurant, it always seemed like it would fall over or someone would knock it over by mistake. I also never knew where to put it when I was riding in the car. All my canes were too big to lay across my lap and too tall to stand up, so I'd have to stick it behind the seat or try to wedge it in next to one of my legs. I used to get aggravated, but now I'm used to it. In fact, I kind of like carrying a cane. If I'm walking down the street with a cane, no one's going to try to steal my purse, right? Holly agrees and says she wants to borrow a cane the next time she goes to New York—here we go again with her borrowing my stuff.

Besides, it looks kind of cool to carry a cane. I picture Charlie Chaplin or those tap dancers from the '40s with their top hats and canes, and I think, maybe I'll start a new trend.

Chapter 11

Three Chords

A few years ago, Holly wrote a song called "Mama" and gave it to Mom as a Mother's Day gift. Holly jokes that she didn't have any money to buy her anything nice, so she wrote this song. Mom loved it.

Like the words in most of Holly's songs, the lyrics are so evocative: *Mama, you were smiling when you could've been crying all night . . .* and *. . . You did more good for me than you will ever know, I've seen mothers fill their children's hearts with hate, but you knew better than to drag me down with you, you let me love my daddy just the same.* I especially love the line, *Then you taught us all about the power of forgiveness . . .*

It's an awesome tribute to our mom and other single moms who never turned bitter or kept their kids from loving their dads. We were all excited when "Mama" became a single on Holly's 2009 album, *Here With Me.*

Right around the time the record was released, Holly was scheduled to perform at the Bluebird Café, the small, prestigious Nashville club, where Garth Brooks and many others were discovered. Mom was in the audience that night, and when it came time for Holly to sing "Mama," she surprised Mom by calling her up on stage. "Hey, y'all, my mama's here tonight," Holly said. "I'm going to have her come up and do harmony on this song."

You should have seen Mom's face. It was priceless. She did great, and afterward we were laughing when she said, "It's a good thing I've been listening to this record and singing along with it at home. What would I have done if I didn't know the words?"

Some people from Holly's record label saw the impromptu performance at the Bluebird and invited Mom to join Holly to record the song for a CMT (Country Music Television) spot the next day.

Mom said she was nervous because they put her on a stool right next to Holly, instead of in the background where most backup singers would normally go. Also, there were no rehearsals. They just got right to it. And Mom was so critical of herself. "I looked seventy years old!" she said. "It was like beauty and the beast."

Well, Mom looked great and she sounded perfect.

Obviously the record company agreed because they invited her to do several more appearances with Holly, including her performance on *The Tonight Show* with Conan O'Brien. That was so exciting! Mom and Holly flew to California and got to the set and ran through the song several times. Mom was nervous because, even though the show was going to be taped, they treat it like a live run-through. In other words, if you mess up, you keep going. No editing.

Right before they went on, Mom looked out into the studio audience, but it was dark so she couldn't see anyone. Then a producer reminded her there were going to be eight million people watching.

When Conan said, "Our special guest is Holly Williams and tonight, her mother, Becky, will be singing with her . . . " Mom says she just froze. They started the song, and even though she managed to start singing, she just stood there like a soldier. Then halfway through, she thought, "I've got to move!" So she started swaying back and forth just a little bit as she sang.

Mom got a couple more chances to perform the song Holly wrote about her. One of the most memorable was when, a few weeks after the *Tonight Show* appearance, Holly made her debut at the Grand Ole Opry. The theme that night was Opry Classics, and they wanted her to sing one Hank Jr. song and one Hank Sr. song, so she sang "Dinosaur" and "I'm So Lonesome I Could Cry." Then she invited Mom onstage to sing "Mama"—again as a surprise. I think this time Mom was ready, though.

For obvious reasons, "Mama" is one of my favorite of my sister's songs. She's written so many over the years. She almost always writes them by herself and she writes them fast. She always did.

When we were really young, Holly kept a notebook called *Holly's Song Folder*, where she would write lyrics or poems or ideas. There she was, eight and nine years old, writing deep, introspective stuff on topics she didn't have a clue about. Her first official composition was "Who Am I," a song about a broken marriage that she thought would be perfect for Debbie Gibson or Tiffany to sing.

Although Holly took voice and piano lessons for a while— we both did—she put songwriting aside for a few years. Other teenage pursuits such as gymnastics, modeling, and going out with her friends took center stage for a while. But when she was seventeen, I showed her how to play three chords on the guitar. And you know what they say about three chords . . .

I'd been taking guitar lessons, so I just showed her the basics. Then, in one afternoon, she wrote three songs, this time with both lyrics and melody. The first complete song she wrote was "My Old Friend Bill," which told the story of Bill Dyer, my dad's dear friend and longtime fishing and hunting buddy, who had recently died of cancer.

I remember Holly going downstairs to get Mom and bringing her up to the playroom so she could play it for her. Later, when Dad came over, Holly handed him a copy of the lyrics. "You've got a gift for words," Dad said. "I think you can do this." That meant so much to her. From then on, Dad was totally supportive of her career. When she saw that Holly was serious, Mom soon came around, too.

Years later, Holly made a demo recording of "My Friend Bill," and I sang backup. She used to play it when she'd do her small gigs around town in restaurants, Irish pubs, and anywhere that would let her play. Although it's never made it onto one of her records, the song is still a sentimental family favorite to this day.

Naturally, Holly's songwriting has evolved over the years. So many of her songs are incredibly deep and thoughtful; sometimes they're drawn from her own experiences, and sometimes they are not. Often, when people listen to Holly's intense lyrics or hear her play some of her more emotional songs, they assume she's this serious, brooding girl. That is so funny to me because she is the exact opposite of a suicidal songwriter, sitting alone in a dark room. A lot of her songs are slow or midtempo, but she's anything but. In fact, one night after a show in Virginia, this man came up to her and said, "Ms. Williams, I just feel your pain."

Holly didn't know what to say to the guy. She didn't want him to think she didn't identify with what she was singing about, but how do you tell someone, "You know, it's just a song. It isn't about me. It doesn't kill me to sing it."

Early 2010, when Holly was playing some shows in Europe, Mom and I met her in London and then traveled with her to Zurich for a couple of shows at the Albisgütli Country Music Festival. Before the first show, which was in a clubhouse-ballroom kind of place, the promoter came up to Holly and said, "We really want people to line dance tonight!"

That cracked me up. I wonder if the guy had ever even heard one of Holly's records. He certainly had never seen one of her shows, where she sits behind the mic and tells stories between songs.

But Holly was a great sport, and that night she played just about every up-tempo cover song she knew. She even called me on stage to sing with her during "Move it On Over." I thought it was so cool how much country music fans in Europe love Hank Sr.'s songs. People we met in Germany and England knew so much about him. It was as if he was still alive and well and topping the charts. They seem to know my grandfather's songs even more than my father's songs, which surprised both Holly and me.

When Holly was starting out in Nashville, often she'd keep it under the radar that she was Hank Jr.'s daughter. She wanted to make her own way and also squelch the inevitable comparisons and expectations.

During the first string of radio interviews she did, the DJs would often say, "Whoa, you're not what we expected at all," meaning they thought a young, female Bocephus would come flying through the door.

Thankfully, no one has ever pressured either Holly or me to become a clone of our father. First of all, as Holly often points out, that would be impossible because we're female. So we get a pass in that sense. But even though we're girls, people could have pushed us to play more rowdy, Bocephus-inspired Gretchen Wilson–type of music.

Don't get me wrong. We both really like Gretchen Wilson's music. In fact, me, Holly, a bunch of my friends, and I (and Dad, too!) were in the crowd scene for her video for "All Jacked Up."

But our music is just different. My voice is more pop rock. People have flattered me when they've said I sound like Sheryl Crow, Sarah McLachlan, or Patty Griffin, or even a young Bonnie Raitt. Holly is the folk singer-songwriter, playing in theaters to audiences who want to hear the words.

We're different from each other and we're different from Dad. Isn't that the way it's supposed to be?

Although I like to take full credit for Holly's career because I taught her to play the G, D, and C chords on guitar, Holly got her inspiration from a lot of sources. There was Dad as well as all the records she would listen to constantly, ranging from the Beatles and Led Zeppelin to Bob Dylan and Radiohead.

I also have to admit that she and I both got at least a little bit of musical inspiration from our stepfather, Johnny Christopher, who was in our lives for a few years. Johnny was an A-list session guitar player who played on dozens of Nashville records in the 1970s and '80s. He was also part of that Memphis bunch that played on all the Elvis Presley songs in the '60s and '70s. Johnny is a great songwriter, too. He is probably best known for cowriting "Always on My Mind," which Brenda Lee and Elvis recorded before Willie Nelson took it to the top. Even the Pet Shop Boys later took a stab at that song.

Anyway, when I was thirteen and Holly was eleven, Mom met Johnny at church. They started dating and got married a couple of months later. It happened really fast, and I wasn't crazy about the whole situation. But looking back, I realize that Mom must have been really lonely. She hadn't dated anyone since she and Dad separated, so I'm sure meeting Johnny was a bright spot for her.

Both Holly and I were entering those teenage years when we'd be living our own lives and going out with our own friends. Mom knew she'd be alone a lot more, so I'm sure she wanted some companionship. Plus it probably entered her mind that having a man around the house when she had two teenagers to deal with wouldn't be a bad idea.

It was a big adjustment bringing someone new into our lives. It had always been just the three of us, and now there was another person. And it was a man.

Holly and I were respectful of Johnny. I only remember one big fight between him and Holly. Mom had asked him to step in and be more of a disciplinarian, which he did—just that one time.

Mostly, we kind of left each other alone—except when it came to food. Johnny was really into organic nutrition and vitamins, and I will admit we learned some things from him. But sometimes, he could be overly direct with his opinions. I remember him getting after me for drinking diet soda, telling me Nutrasweet was so bad for me. Well, it was hard being a fourteen-year-old with diabetes who couldn't drink regular Cokes. I didn't want to have to give up Diet Cokes, too.

Although Johnny and Dad really didn't interact very much, when they did, they were polite to each other. They got along fine. But when I told Dad about the Nutrasweet lecture, he immediately ordered several cases of Diet Coke and had them delivered to our house. Johnny didn't say a word.

To this day, Aunt Jo Lynn tells that story and never fails to bring us all to tears from laughing so hard.

Now that I've got some distance, I'm thinking it must have been hard for Johnny to come into a house with two teenage girls who he really didn't know. I don't think we behaved badly, although once, when he made me mad, I went up to my room and blasted one of Dad's records as loud as I could. On the positive side, though, Johnny taught both Holly and me some guitar chords, and I remember him taking time to help me with my English papers, which I appreciated.

Ultimately, things didn't work out between him and Mom, and although I was sad for her, I couldn't hide the fact that, in my opinion, he never appreciated her enough. I thought she deserved better.

For the most part, their split was amicable. When Johnny left—I know this sounds selfish—I felt like we got our mom back. I was excited that, once again, it would be just the three of us girls.

After I finished high school, I decided to go to college at Belmont University in Nashville, just a few miles from the house where I grew up. Even though it was so close to home, I moved into the dorms my freshman year and started school.

My goal was to get into the music business program, but it's extremely competitive. They require a really high GPA. I wasn't a terrible student, but I hate taking tests. I'm not naturally book smart, although people tell me I have good common sense. I've noticed that a lot of people who are book smart are dumb as rocks when it comes to common sense.

Anyway, Brentwood Academy, where I went to high school, was a challenging, private school and I had to work really hard. I had learning disabilities as a kid, so my whole life, if I slacked off, I'd fall behind right away. From ninth to twelfth grade, I had a tutor, Mrs. Bunch, to help me with homework and to prepare me for tests. She was such a sweetheart and she saved me.

When I got to Belmont, I took general studies at first. I liked it there and I made some really good friends; I was even in a sorority for a while. But I kind of felt like I wasn't getting the best college experience. Belmont is more of a suitcase college, where kids go home on the weekends. Because I'd been in Nashville most of my life, I started to think I needed to try somewhere and something new.

For as long as I can remember, I loved fashion and my taste in clothes was very specific. When I was really small, maybe three or four years old, I insisted on wearing cowboy boots everywhere. Even in the summertime, I'd wear shorts, a polo shirt, and these grey alligator cowboy boots. In preschool, I'd lay out my outfits the night before, making sure everything matched, including the color of my hair bows. Growing up, most of my part-time jobs were in clothing stores. That's hardly unusual for a teenage girl, but I really thought I had a knack for the designing and business part of things.

I started thinking about fashion. Then, while watching the Miss Teen USA Pageant on TV, I saw an ad for Bauder College, a fashion merchandising school in Atlanta. I thought it looked really cool, and Atlanta was away from home but not so far away—and certainly not as big and scary—as New York City or Los Angeles. So I went to Atlanta.

It sounds kind of strange, but Bauder College actually used to be located under Phipps Plaza, the big mall in Atlanta's Buckhead neighborhood, though the school has its own building now. To be more specific, the campus formerly sat directly underneath Lord & Taylor, which I guess makes sense for a fashion merchandizing school. The students ate lunch at the mall all the time, and if we needed to do research on a trend or take a field trip for a class, there were dozens of high-end retailers right upstairs.

During my first year at Bauder, I lived in a condo with six other girls. The dorms had burned down, so the university bought these condos that were built in the 1970s and turned them into pseudo-dorms. It was fun living with five other girls; there were three bedrooms, so we bunked two to a room. The only challenge was that there was one bathroom for all six of us.

The student body at Bauder was almost 100 percent female, although there were a few males—mostly gay guys—in our class. I got very close to one of the guys, Dusty, and we were really excited when a modeling agency in town asked the two of us to work at a charity fashion show connected with the Super Bowl that year. The game was being played in Atlanta and it was really cool for us because our hometown Tennessee Titans were one of the teams. But as far as we were concerned, the fashion show was an even better draw than the game. It was a big breast cancer awareness benefit featuring a lot of big stars, and our job would be to help them get dressed for the runway.

Holly drove over from Nashville to help out, and right away, she was assigned to dress Niki Taylor, who was really nice. Dusty got assigned to Star Jones (when she was "big Star Jones"), and I felt bad for him because she was not so nice. I dressed Jason Sehorn, the former NY Giants player who is married to Angie Harmon, and he couldn't have been more polite. He kept saying, "Thank you so much" over and over every time I helped him with his jacket or handed him a different shirt to change into.

That night, we went out to a Super Bowl party at a club rented out by Wyclef Jean. Kid Rock was there, and that's the night Holly and I met him for the first time. Many music fans know that Dad and Kid Rock, or Bobby, as Dad always calls him, are good friends. They hunt and fish together all the time, and there was even a rumor going around for a while that Bobby was Dad's illegitimate son, which was sparked by the line, "I've been hanging out with my rebel son, Kid Rock . . . " in the song "The F Word," which they recorded together in 2002. Well, Bobby and Dad are not related, but we do think of him as family these days. He sang at Holly's wedding and we see and talk to him all the time. But as far as I know, the night Holly and I met him, he and Dad didn't know each other yet.

So we're in this club, which we'd gotten into with our fake IDs. I was only one month shy of being twenty-one, so I don't feel too bad about that. Inside, we saw Kid Rock at one of the tables. We'd just read an interview in *Rolling Stone* in which he talked about being a huge fan of Dad's, so Holly went up to him and introduced herself.

They talked for a while, then Holly came over and grabbed me off the dance floor where I was dancing with my friends, saying, "C'mon! Kid Rock wants to meet you."

So we went over and hung out with him. The next time I saw Dad, I said, "This Kid Rock guy loves you . . . " Now the feeling is mutual.

My time at Bauder flew by. The math classes were a breeze because I'd already struggled through the hard stuff at Brentwood Academy and at Belmont. I loved the textiles classes, where we learned about fabrics and how clothes are made. The teacher gave us cool, practical tips that I still use; for instance, never use dryer sheets because they break down the fibers of your clothes and can cause them to get moldy.

I also liked the marketing classes, especially the one in which we had to come up with a concept for our own business. My idea for a business was *Long Lines*, a line of clothes for tall women. I've wanted to do this ever since I was in the seventh grade and had to go around wearing pants that were too short because Mom couldn't find any long enough for me.

As I was finishing my first year at Bauder, Holly was getting ready to graduate from high school. She had visited the University of Alabama and was seriously thinking about going there. Then she changed her mind. Instead of going to college, she would take a year or two off and pursue music full time.

Mom was not very happy about that.

When Holly broke the news, Mom said, "Well, Holly, you'd better learn to say, 'Would you like fries with that?'"

Even though we come from a family of musicians, Mom knew that neither Holly nor I could just walk out there and cash in on our name. There would be a lot of hard work and possibly heartbreak. There were no guarantees.

She wanted us to be able to support ourselves. Plus Mom worried about Holly taking up the life of a road musician. It was an unstable life and full of temptations. But Holly is a great saleswoman, and she told Mom, "If I go to college now I'll just party and goof off and waste your money."

It didn't take long for Mom—and, later, Dad—to see that Holly was serious and this was the right choice for her.

Immediately, she got internships at Curb Records and Sony Publishing so she could meet some people and learn more about the music business. Then, while working behind the make-up counter at the Green Hills Mall by day, she started playing in clubs around Nashville at night. There are so many places in and around town where aspiring singer songwriters can try out their material. You don't get paid much, if at all, but it's great practice. What's more, there's no better way to learn your craft and develop a seriously thick skin than playing in bars where maybe three people are listening to you.

During this time—when she was eighteen, nineteen, and twenty—Holly says she really found her voice. Singing had never come naturally to her. She always tells the story of when she tried out for the high school chorus four years in a row and never made it. But the more she practiced, the more she could stay on pitch and the more motivated she became to perform her own original songs in public.

After I graduated from Bauder, I came back to Nashville and worked at different retail stores while I tried to figure out what I wanted to do. I still had music on my mind, but even though I was starting to write songs with people in Nashville, after a year or so, I felt like my career and my life needed a jump start. So I decided to move to Los Angeles.

I thought Los Angeles would be the perfect place for me. It's a fashion capital and, as far as music goes, there were a lot more songwriters and producers making pop music—the kind of music I was interested in doing—than there were in Nashville. Holly had stayed out there for a while and had a mostly positive experience—except for the dozens of parking tickets. Plus the weather is great. And, in the interest of full disclosure, there was also this boy that I was seeing who had moved out there.

So I packed up and went.

I planned to make some connections and write music with other songwriters, but before I did anything, I needed a job. I responded to an ad on Craig's List and got a job at Kitson, a chic boutique on South Robertson Boulevard in Beverly Hills. The store, which was two doors down from the famous celeb-sighting restaurant, The Ivy, was right in the hub of where people go to be seen. Because my job consisted mostly of filling internet orders, I, for one, was rarely seen. I usually sat in the back.

Kitson was one of the trendy shops in that area where celebrities were known to frequent, so the paparazzi pretty much camped outside across the street. Sometimes the photographers would try to follow them in when someone famous meandered through the front door. If a photographer did manage to slip in, one of the clerks would just shoo them out so Nicollette Sheridan or Jessica Alba could poke through all the Marc Jacobs and Isabella Fiore handbags undisturbed.

I remember one day I went outside and saw Nicole Richie and Paris Hilton walking toward the store. They were surrounded by photographers, and one of the guys broke away from the pack and slammed me against the door as he tried to get one last shot of Paris before she ducked inside. It was then that I noticed that the store manager had blacked out all the windows so no one could see Paris and Nicole when they went inside to shop. I guess we were expecting them.

I shouldn't have been surprised by this, but I found most of the people that I met in L.A. to be really superficial. I know. Sometimes it takes me a while to catch on. But seriously, whenever I heard that people in L.A. were phony—especially show business people—I always thought it was just a lazy stereotype. I used to think, well, how do you know that for sure? They can't all be phony.

But while I lived in Los Angeles, I found that to be the case over and over again. I'd meet someone new and they'd say, "Call me if you need anything." Then, I'd call them and they wouldn't call me back.

However, I will say that I met a few nice people out there. The guy topping that list was John Roberts, who was working as Pamela Anderson's assistant. He absolutely saved my life.

When I first got to L.A., I moved into an apartment in West Hollywood with a gay guy I knew from Nashville. (I only mention his sexual orientation so Mom doesn't freak out that I lived with a boy.) The place was great; it was on North Crescent Heights Boulevard, right in the center of everything. The problem was that right after I got there, my roommate skipped town. He said he'd paid the rent for that month already, but that turned out not to be the case. I kept calling him and he didn't return my calls. Naturally, the landlord got annoyed and said that unless I paid the back rent, they were going to evict me.

First, they turned off the hot water. That's where John first came to my rescue by letting me take a hot shower at his house. Then the landlord put a note on the door from a lawyer stating that they were going to keep all my furniture until the back rent was paid. So John came over that night and helped me move out in secret. We took all my stuff to a place in Simi Valley, where a friend of my dad's owned a house. And that's where I stayed, living with the guy's girlfriend and her son.

Thanks to John, I'd escaped the ticked-off landlord. And I never heard from the gay guy from Nashville—still to this day.

Even though I had a decent place to stay, I was a long way from work, and most days, driving on the interstate was like inching my way out of the parking lot after a stadium concert. My commute was two hours each way. Even a good stereo in the car can't ease that kind of pain.

I wasn't loving Los Angeles. I spent half my time in the car. Then one day I parked in the wrong place and my car got towed. I was living hand to mouth. I had barely made any music connections. And to top things off, the boy I was seeing forgot to mention that he had another girlfriend.

Not long after the towed-car/lying-boyfriend fiasco, I was driving to work one day when, just a few minutes into my trip, I turned around and went back to Simi Valley. I packed up and headed back to Nashville. I'm not sure if the people at Kitson noticed that I never came in to work again. They didn't call. And if they had, I wouldn't call them back.

After I was back in Nashville for a while, I went to work at my friend Melody Malloy's store, Bloke. This was such a cool concept: a trendy but comfortable, upscale clothing store for men.

We sold great clothes at Bloke, but guys didn't just come in to check out the latest from Diesel or Martin Gordon. Melody set up bar stools and served Guinness and Jack Daniels for special customers. There was a pool table, a dartboard, and a big TV so guys could watch football games in between trying on shirts and belts. There was a hanging bubble chair and classic rock album covers and pictures of pin-up girls on the wall. The whole place had a retro, guy's guy vibe.

The funny thing was that the place looked a lot like a bar or a coffee shop. When people saw the big "Open 24 hours" neon sign, which was just part of the décor, they'd understandably make that mistake. Sometimes people would even knock on the door late at night, looking to come in to have a beer. But after dark, the store was closed. And more often than not, we were out and about.

The summer of 2005 was one of the best summers ever. My girlfriends and I went to shows and concerts and clubs. We had so many laughs. Like the night Two-Foot Fred tried to kiss me in the car. I said, "Sorry, Fred . . . ," and he said, "Well, you can't blame a guy for trying."

I was so happy to be home.

Chapter 12

One Step Up, Two Steps Back

While I was recovering from the accident and the surgeries that followed, I slept a lot. And while I was sleeping, I often had recurring dreams. One was about my grandfather Warren White, whose funeral I was traveling to that day back in March. This was a comforting dream where I'd see Papaw and we would be walking down the road together or I'd see him doing the everyday things that he used to do before Alzheimer's and Parkinson's really took hold of him, such as driving his tractor or sitting at the kitchen table. I dreamed about him almost every night. Then I'd wake up thinking about him and the picture that always came to mind was Papaw doing his afternoon exercises.

Every afternoon without fail, Papaw used to walk up and down the tall, carpeted stairs in my grandparents' big Louisiana house one hundred times. He was always dressed the same way, in his cowboy boots, khaki pants, and button-down shirt with his wallet in the front pocket and one of his handmade bolos tied at the neck.

Up and down, up and down. That was his exercise and he never missed a day.

I was so happy when Papaw appeared in my dreams. I often wondered why I hadn't seen him in heaven when my spirit left my body after the wreck. My cousin said that because he had just died, he probably hadn't gotten there yet. "Maybe he was still being fitted for his angel wings!" she said.

My other recurring dream was not uplifting at all—just the opposite. This dream was the classic falling dream, where I felt like I was cascading downward and, just before I hit the ground, I'd be jolted awake.

Any pop psychologist could figure out the meaning of these two dreams. Papaw equals comfort and stability and happiness. Falling means insecurity and anxiety and fear. Unfortunately, I often struggled with fear while I was awake.

After taking my first few steps, my next obstacle to overcome was getting behind the wheel of a car again. My beautiful new Mercedes SUV had been sitting in the driveway for months. We'd gone out in it a few times, always with someone other than me driving. At first, I preferred that someone else drive, but then every time a car would honk or come a little too close, my heart would skip a beat. I decided I'd rather be in control. So I took the wheel—for short trips around town, anyway.

As a rule, I tried hard not to allow myself to worry about "what ifs," but one thing I couldn't help being anxious about was my voice. As the doctors tried to reconnect my bones and my mom and my sister helped me heal and my friends tried to cheer me up, I smiled, but secretly I feared that I wouldn't be able to sing again.

Nobody at either Memphis or Vanderbilt hospital told me this was a possibility. In fact, the nurses tried to comfort me, saying that the breathing tubes and medications and other things going in and out of my nose and throat would cause bruising and dryness, but everything would heal with time.

Still, I couldn't help worrying about it.

In the hospital, I'd tried to sing a couple of times with Mom, but nothing came out. Even though I could talk, when I tried to sing, it was as if I had laryngitis. I knew I was being a little crazy, but even when I got home, at first I was afraid to even open my mouth to try.

Besides being scared, I was also reluctant to try to sing because I was so tired and weak. Most people don't think of singing as something that requires physical fitness, but it does. If you can't sit up or if you're having trouble breathing, singing is a real challenge.

A few weeks after I got home, my voice teacher, Phoebe Binkley, came to visit me. Phoebe is well known in Nashville. She started out way back when as a singer in the St. Louis Municipal Opera, and after working in New York for years, she moved to Nashville and concentrated on songwriting, often collaborating with her husband, Bob. They wrote songs for Marty Robbins including "I Don't Care (If You Don't Care for Me)," among many others, and for the last several decades, she has worked with dozens of famous and aspiring singers ranging from Kathy Mattea, the year she won Female Vocalist of the Year, to Reese Witherspoon, who came to Phoebe while preparing to play June Carter Cash in the movie *Walk the Line*.

I first started working with Phoebe when I was nineteen or twenty years old. I had always loved to sing, but the only place I ever did it was in church or at home. I was way too shy to enter the talent show at school or try out for a part in a musical. But even in the safe environments of church and home, where there was really no competition and I never felt as if anyone was judging me, I knew I was holding back.

I'm a quiet person, and back then I was a relatively soft, quiet singer, but I knew I had a strong voice. I could feel it. Singing came naturally to me, and I was blessed with perfect pitch, but I didn't really know how to project. I wanted to figure out how to really let go. So I went to Phoebe for help.

During our first couple of lessons, we worked on some gospel songs that I wanted to sing with Mom. "You've got a really amazing upper register in your voice," Phoebe told me. "And there are a lot of dimensions there."

After a few lessons, I really let loose. It felt so good to sing loud—or not so much loud as strong. It felt powerful and easy all at the same time. I was really encouraged. But that was then.

Now, all these years later as I lay in my bed in the living room, I was feeling incredibly discouraged. If I started working with Phoebe again, as she suggested, it wasn't as if I would be starting from where we left off. Because neither of us knew how the accident had affected my physical ability to sing, we wouldn't even be starting from scratch. I felt as if I was starting at less than zero.

So Phoebe came back to visit me, and she completely made my day when she gave me a beautiful amethyst healing stone that her friend and former student Crystal Gayle gave her when Phoebe was recovering from surgery a few years ago.

Phoebe understands overcoming physical obstacles. She had polio when she was eight years old and has dealt with the repercussions of the disease her entire life. Maybe that's why she knew it was crucial to my spirit to try to sing even though, at that point, I could barely even sit up in bed.

I agreed to try a few lessons while I was laid up. She teased me, saying that she wasn't normally in the business of making house calls. "This is the only time I've been to somebody's house to give them voice lessons," she said, "besides Charlie Daniels."

We started by doing some of the exercises I already knew, such as bubbling, where you make the sound of a boat motor with your mouth, or panting, which is basically heavy breathing. Then together, we made a series of other sounds: Shh! Shh! Shh! Huh! Huh! Huh! After fifteen minutes or so, I had to quit. All the breathing and huffing and puffing made me unbelievably dizzy. My energy level dipped and I had to rest.

But I kept practicing, doing some of those exercises every day. Then I'd do little things, such as biting the sides of my mouth or my tongue to stimulate saliva or I'd suck on glycerin tablets to soothe my throat. By the time Phoebe came back again a few weeks later, I was able to get into my wheelchair and sit next to her at Mom's piano. When Phoebe hit a note, hmmmmm, I would match it with my voice. I'd hold the note until I couldn't hold it anymore. Then, she would hit one note higher, hmm-mmm, and I would match it again.

I kept catching myself holding my breath, so we practiced breathing a lot. "Push your stomach out, Hilary," Phoebe said. "Like a hot air balloon. You don't breathe in . . . "

She explained to me that the muscles in my abdomen and diaphragm and throat had been damaged, but they weren't gone. The network of muscles was still there. Like the rest of my rehab, it was just a matter of building everything back up.

So we kept going. We'd go up and down the scales—wa, wa, wa, wa, wa, wa, wa, wa—a few times. Then she'd have me sing "Deck the Halls," several times (which cracked me up because it was summertime), beginning in a low key and ratcheting up a little higher each time I began a new round. Phoebe sang a note for me and said, "Here's where you are now. Next time, we'll go a little bit further."

I pushed and pushed and practiced in between Phoebe's visits. How annoying that must have been for Mom. It must have been like having a teenager at home practicing his new trombone.

As I sang the scales and cracked my way through the high Cs, I wondered, where did those old notes go? I wanted them back, all the notes I used to sing. I wanted to build them up and stock-pile them and keep them ready for when I would light their fuse and let them all go again.

After a few months, when I could leave the house, I started once again going to Phoebe's home in Brentwood for my lessons. I didn't find this out until much later, but before I came over, she would make sure that the porch light was on and that there was space for me to park right by the door. She made sure the lights were turned on in the hallway and that anything that could have potentially blocked my path was out of the way.

We always worked in her piano room, where the wood-paneled walls were covered with signed pictures of her past and current clients. She'd lead me to a big, comfortable, broad-backed chair (most clients stand up for their lessons), and then she would lean over and pull the chain on the little Tiffany lamp on top of her piano to throw some light on her keyboard. Then we would begin: Wa, wa, wa, wa, wa, wa . . .

Soon, we were back to where I'd started, and after a few months, I felt as though I'd hit the point where we left off. "It's cumulative, Hilary," Phoebe would say. "It's a journey. There has to be joy in the journey."

I sang the National Anthem, something I have never done in public. How funny to be singing that song in Phoebe's little room. After that, she had me sing arias from Italian operas, which I loved doing. Then Phoebe gave me a gift I loved even more than the healing stone she got from Crystal Gayle: "I think you've come back, Hilary," she said. "Stronger. I think you've come back even stronger."

Almost a year after the accident, life was improving steadily. On good days, I was up and walking with a cane. On bad days, I'd use crutches or a walker or a wheelchair or I would just stay at home, resting in bed or on the couch. I was still doing physical therapy, although not as frequently. I still had things to work on, including the torn ligaments in my knees and the rebuilding of muscle memory everywhere, especially my ankle, which seemed to always want to turn to the side as if the external fixator were still holding it in place.

One thing that always made me feel better was a visit from the massage therapist. I'd always loved massages—who doesn't? But when my friend Laurie's ex-husband Scott came over to give me my first massage after weeks in bed, I can only try to describe how amazing that was. When someone moves parts of you that you can't move yourself and—physically, gently—pushes toxins from sore, nonworking muscles, it is nothing short of sublime.

After those first couple of sessions, I began working with another massage therapist, Barbara Bane, who introduced me to Young Living essential oils and the healing power of aromatherapy.

I still have problems with pain in my legs and, especially, in my feet, which tend to cramp up when I favor one side or the other when I walk. Every time Barbara goes to work on those knots, at first I want to jump off the table. But then, when she's done, I feel as though someone hit a giant reset button and set my body straight.

Much of my therapy during this time was in the pool, which I absolutely loved. Because I no longer needed a wheelchair lift to get in and out of the water, Karen and I often met at Athena, a day spa in Brentwood that has a gorgeous European-style pool. Sometimes Karen would get in the pool with me and sometimes she would coach me from the side.

I just loved walking or running in the pool, where I could use my body to make my own resistance. The pain seemed to almost disappear in the water. And we'd cap off every session with a trip to the sauna or whirlpool. This wasn't like work at all.

So things were moving along. Then, in early February, a guy I met a few years before called me unexpectedly. "Hey, it's a blast from your past!" he said. "Want to go to lunch?"

Dating was really the last thing on my mind. February is kind of a downer month in Nashville. Usually it's really gray and gloomy out—cold enough to be miserable but not quite cold enough for it to snow. I was feeling kind of low. And I wasn't feeling very attractive, to say the least. I still had a lot of broken parts and I looked like a cripple when I walked. The last thing I felt was pretty. I felt like I was damaged goods. But the appeal of going out won out over self-pity. I said yes.

A few days later, I met Keven, or "Big Kev" as everybody called him, for lunch at P. F. Chang's. It was a complete coincidence, but the day we went out just happened to be Valentine's Day.

When we got to the restaurant, Big Kev handed me a card, a little stuffed dog with a heart in its mouth, and some sugar-free candy—extra points for not giving regular candy to a person with diabetes.

I was really surprised that he did that.

"Oh no!" I said. "I have nothing for you."

He was sweet and easy to talk to, and it was such a boost to know that a guy liked me. I thought he was cute, too. What's more, the fact that he was a rock-and-roll type guy, all covered with tattoos, made me less self-conscious about the way I looked. I figured that a guy like that wasn't going to be too superficial.

I first met Big Kev a few years back at the Academy of Country Music Awards in Los Angeles when he was working as Kid Rock's personal assistant. I was staying in Dad's room, helping take care of Katie and Sam, and a bunch of us were hanging out when my stepmother, Mary Jane, announced in front of everyone, "Hilary, you need a boyfriend!"

Big Kev piped up, "I'd date you."

I appreciated the compliment and the diversion from unwanted attention from Mary Jane, but Keven was seeing somebody else at the time. So, although I saw him from time to time at Bobby's shows, we mostly went our separate ways.

Years later, when we started dating, Keven was working as a bus driver for different artists; he was with Keith Anderson when we first got together. Dating a driver is kind of tough because drivers stay up all night to drive from city to city when they're on the job. Then they sleep all day. So on days off, they still tend to stay up all night and sleep all day. It's hard to switch back to normal. But for the most part, he was great company and we had a lot of fun together.

In July of that year, life ground to a halt for me again when I went in for another major surgery, this one to fix my right femur (thigh bone). Dr. Kregor knew this operation was coming. In Memphis, the doctors put in a nail down the center of the bone to hold everything together, but it wasn't healing. Doctor Kregor wanted to give me time to recover after my hip replacement on my left side before I went for major surgery on my right side. It's really hard on a patient when you can't put weight on either leg. Then you're basically bedridden. But in June I started having a lot of pain in the area from my right hip to my right knee, so we scheduled the operation.

During this particular procedure, Dr. Kregor removed the old nails and screws, and then he inserted a metal plate that would ultimately, when it healed, fix the "femoral non-union." He also removed the plate from my right ankle. Lose a plate, gain a plate, I always say.

When you hear that someone has a plate in their leg or their hip or their ankle, you probably imagine something shaped like a Frisbee or a tea cup saucer. But the plate I have in my leg doesn't look like that. It's more like a rod, although it's not cylindrical like a flag pole. It's a flat-looking plate with holes in it. And it's really skinny, maybe an inch wide, and it extends all the way from my hip down to my knee.

And yes, it does make it tough to go through airport security. The alarms would definitely go off if I tried to walk through the scanner in the regular line. I always have to call ahead and arrange for a special screening. I also bring little wallet-sized laminated pictures of all my X-rays that Traci, Dr. Kregor's nurse, made for me so I can prove that the metal I am "carrying" could not be used as a weapon. That usually does the trick.

Anyway, to facilitate the healing of my femur, Dr. Kregor had to begin the surgery by doing extensive bone grafts. The plate had to have something to attach onto, so he basically had to scrape bone from somewhere else—in this case, the back side of my pelvis—then attach it to the femur before he installed the plate. If my body cooperated and everything healed, I would have this plate in my leg forever.

The good news was that after the surgery, I had extensive range of motion in my knees and hips almost immediately. It hurt a lot to move them, but it was great to have things working again. The other good news was that once again, my legs were nearly even. The medical notes said, "Patient had a good correction of leg length." That was something I never thought I'd care about, but I looked forward to standing up and seeing for myself.

The bad news was that standing up would be difficult. I would need to go through the exact same steps I did when I previously relearned to walk. It was hard to think of it this way, but I would need to re-relearn to walk—all over again.

The steps would be the same and I couldn't skip a single one. Things would feel different this time, though, so I'd have to compensate for the changes and shifts in my body. Instead of putting my weight on my right leg when standing up or taking my first steps, I'd put my weight on my left leg. This time, I'd have to try not to limp to the left rather than the right.

The thought of going through all those steps again didn't bother me so much as reverting to my other postoperative routines. I was back to sleeping in the bed in Mom's living room, back to spending most of the day in bed, and back to using the piece of pantyhose-covered plywood to slide from the bed to the Porta-Potty.

That part was demoralizing.

Trying to be helpful, some people would say to me, "Well, you've been through this before. So you know what to do! This time it will be easier on you."

I guess there was some truth to that.

However, when you've been through something difficult or painful and you know that you're facing it all over again, I think it may be worse the second time around. The first time, you don't really know what things are going to feel like and be like, so you can hope for the best or, at least, manage to block it all out.

But when you've been there, you can't deny what's coming.

Think of a guy who goes sailing on the ocean when a big storm comes along and capsizes his boat. He spends hours and hours in the freezing cold ocean, holding on to the overturned boat all night. Then, when the boat sinks, he manages to tread water until he is rescued the next day.

How do you think that guy would feel if he got up the courage to go sailing again and his boat overturned for the second time? Do you think he would be calm and say, "Oh well, I've only got fourteen hours to go with no water and hopefully no sharks will come, and I didn't die of exposure last time, so . . . " I don't think he would be calm at all. I think the guy would know what he was in for and freak out.

Maybe that's a little overdramatic. The fact was that I did know the drill. Mom's nursing skills were great by this time and, unbelievably, her attitude was so positive and cheerful despite the fact that she was looking at another three or four months when she could barely leave the house.

We had our routine down, and this time around, I had Keven to help.

It's not exactly your typical dating scenario, but because I was comfortable around him, he often helped me with things. He'd help prop me up or go get me a pillow or go to the drugstore to pick up my prescriptions. And sometimes he'd even help me with highly embarrassing, personal things like going to the bathroom. He'd lift me onto the chair and I'd put a towel over myself while he'd leave the room as I did my business. Then he'd come back, help me back up into bed, and go dump the bucket. Not exactly the stuff of romance novels!

Even when I was still in my wheelchair, Keven drove me around a lot, to doctor's appointments, to the mall, or out to eat. When I felt a little bit better, we'd even occasionally go out at night, although he really had to talk me into doing that. A few times, we went out to Loser's, the club near Music Row. We'd take the small wheelchair, the one we could fold up, and once we got inside, Keven would put the wheelchair away and I'd move onto a barstool.

I know Keven meant well, and it was great seeing people I hadn't seen in a long time, but I felt very self-conscious being there. Looking back, it probably wasn't the best idea.

Most of the time, we just hung out or did ordinary things like going out to lunch or running errands. Even when I was using a walker, crutches, or my canes, sometimes I'd use those electric wheelchair-carts they have at Target. It was impossible to shop

with a walker, crutches, or a cane because I couldn't reach for anything. Forget holding a bag. But if I rode in the cart, I could put
stuff in the little basket and give my legs a break at the same time.
I know I looked kind of ridiculous riding in that cart; Keven used
to say, do you have to use that thing? It was embarrassing, especially when it started making that loud beeping noise when I put
it in reverse.

As much as I might have liked to, we hardly ever went to the
movies the whole time I was in the wheelchair because the handicapped section is located in the very first row. Whoever decided
to put that section right in front of the screen didn't consider the
fact that people in wheelchairs may not be able to crane their
neck backward during an entire movie. I did go to the movies,
though, to see *Cars* with my friend Angela and her cousin, who
was visiting from Germany where he was stationed in the army.
Angela's cousin was so sweet. He picked me up and carried me up
the stairs and put me in a regular seat.

And another time I went to the movies with Mom and Holly. It
was the premiere of *Flicka*, Tim McGraw's cowboy movie. It was
kind of a big deal in Nashville, and there was a big party at the Bel-
court Theater where Tim and Faith Hill and other celebrities
walked the red carpet. We were excited because Holly had a song,
"Rodeo Road," on the soundtrack and I really wanted to be there.

One of the best parts of that night for me was meeting Tim
and Faith's cook, Zeny, a wonderful woman from Hawaii. Tim
and Faith had already sent food to our house after the accident—
all of it amazing and all of it made by Zeny. After meeting her at
the premier, she and I became friends; she even took me out for
sushi. And even better, every time I had a surgery, a few days later
Zeny would send over these awesome home-cooked dishes made
with fresh vegetables from Tim and Faith's garden.

I used to try to hide the food from everybody else, stashing a
little in the freezer so I could eat it when I got my appetite back.

I still wish I had some of those recipes, but when I asked her for some of them, Zeny said, "I don't have any! I just cook."

As the weeks passed after my last surgery, things were slowly getting back to normal—well, my new definition of normal, anyway. I'd completed weeks of therapy, beginning with Karen lifting me by the belt to a sitting position over and over until the vertigo stopped. Then we went to the pool to do exercises. Then I stood up. Then I put weight on my left leg, and finally, I put weight on my new and improved right leg. I went from bed to wheelchair to walker to crutches to canes and, finally, to where I was using one cane.

I moved back upstairs to my old room again and returned to using the upstairs bathroom that still had the medical chair in the shower and some new handicapped handrails on the sides of the tub. Things were good.

Then, in February (what is it about February in Nashville?), almost seven months after the surgery to install the plate in my right leg, I started having a lot of pain. At first I thought maybe I just pulled a muscle. Maybe I've been walking too much or exercising too hard? Even though the pain was directly surrounding the plate running from hip to thigh, I did my best to explain it away. I mean, I always had some kind of pain, so maybe this would go away.

Then one morning, Dad met Keven and me for breakfast at Noshville, a great deli near Broadway. After we ate, we took a drive over to Corner Music, a small shop on 12th Avenue South full of guitars, amps, keyboards, and other goodies for hard-core musicians. The place has been there since 1976, and the session players in town know it well. So does Dad, evidently, because he walked right in and began picking up guitars and playing them one by one.

He was having a blast! And the guys who were working there, the only other people in the shop besides us, thought it was hilarious.

Dad picked up a custom Fender and strummed it for a little while. Then he picked up a Gibson with a solid spruce top and started playing "Wipe Out," that cool old Surfaris instrumental from the 1960s. "Man, I used to play a guitar just like this when I was Rockin' Randall back in high school!" he said, as he moved his fingers up and down the frets.

We were having so much fun. I tried not to show how bad I was hurting. I just sat there wincing and forcing myself to smile.

The next day, I met Keven for lunch at Baja Fresh. When I got out of the car, I could barely walk. The pain was excruciating; it felt as though a Roman candle was shooting off inside my leg right next to my thigh bone. And worst of all, my leg felt wobbly; it actually felt as if it was coming loose.

I got back in the car but I knew I couldn't drive, so Keven took me home. I called Dr. Kregor, but he was in Cancun teaching for the next five days. So I went in to see his colleague, Dr. Erika Mitchell.

"You've broken your plate, Hilary," she said.

I was stunned. "What?" I said. "You mean . . . Did I do something to cause this?"

"No, no," she said. "The bone just couldn't take the pressure, so the plate snapped."

My first reaction was anger. The plate was supposed to last forever—a lifetime. And now it just snaps? Just like that?

Dad felt mad at first, too. "What?" he said. "They need to cut you open again?"

When I called Mom to tell her the news, she was just devastated. She said that besides the call she got the day of the accident, this was the worst phone call she's ever received. I hated calling her with this news. I still remember her crying on the phone.

It was just so depressing and confusing and frustrating. If the plate was supposed to last forever, what went wrong? If these things really don't last forever, and now we knew that they didn't, what are the chances this will happen again? Was this anyone's fault? Could anything have prevented this? And what happens now?

I knew I was in for another major surgery and another three- to six-month rehabilitation. After that, I would need to relearn to walk. Again.

Chapter 13

Mending

The failure of the blade plate in my right leg was nobody's fault. The piece of titanium wasn't defective. I hadn't put undo strain on it by exercising too much. I hadn't kept the bone from healing by exercising too little. And there were no problems with Dr. Kregor's surgical technique. The plate just broke. It was demoralizing for everyone, including Dr. Kregor.

As he explained, bone is stronger than titanium, stainless steel, or cobalt chrome, the materials normally used to make a plate. If the bone doesn't heal and adhere properly to the plate, it can push on it and force it to snap. That's what happened to me.

Dr. Kregor has a greater than 95 percent success rate on this type of surgery. Only a handful of his patients have had their femoral plates fail. I couldn't dwell on the fact that probably due to my diabetes, which slows healing, or the severity of my injuries, I became one of the unlucky 5 percent.

I was dreading the next operation, but it needed to be done—and soon. I could feel metal moving around in my body. There was nothing to do but try again.

So on February 12, 2008, I checked back into Vanderbilt Hospital for what would be my twenty-third surgery since the accident. Before they came in to wheel me into the operating room, I remember Dad standing at my bedside and trying to make me laugh. "Twenty-three operations!" he said, shaking his head. "You beat me! I only had nine."

During the procedure, Dr. Kregor removed the broken plate, performed a bone graft, and reinserted a new femoral blade plate with additional screws. Every time I heard the doctor put in additional screws, I couldn't help but feel like the handyman special. Maybe later I could put myself up for sale on Craig's List under the "Fixer Upper" category.

Anyway, when Dr. Kregor closed me up, he had a plastic surgeon sew me up with clear stitching so the scars wouldn't be so bad. I thought that was really thoughtful.

The surgery was a success, but as with the previous operation, there were no guarantees that this plate would last forever. However, I thought, what are the chances that a plate could break twice? That's got to be almost impossible, right? Then I decided I didn't want to know.

When I got back home to Mom's house and started the rehab process again, besides working to strengthen my leg, I had to work hard on accepting what had happened and believing that it wouldn't happen again. There were scientific reasons why the plate was more likely to heal this time around, including the fact that Dr. Kregor put in a lot of extra bone and extra screws to stabilize the plate. But it also had to be about faith.

Mom was a great inspiration to me during this time. Her conviction never wavered. I remember watching her as she went about her duties, putting a pillow between my knees before she gently rolled me over to change my sheets. She had gotten so good at this. Maybe it was a little easier this time around; I no longer had cracked ribs or an open wound on my leg. But still, she had to be careful of my stitches and my delicate right side.

"Mom, I'm sorry you have to do all this," I said.

"I wouldn't want anybody else to do it," she replied.

Mom knew things would get better—she absolutely knew it—and her strong belief spilled over to me and reinforced my own faith whenever I felt it starting to slip away. Although I felt sad and anxious and disheartened about having to go through this second surgery, I never felt mad—not at God anyway. Yes, I was angry and aggravated when the plate first snapped. But I never felt as if I was being singled out or punished. Although those kinds of thoughts did slip into my mind briefly immediately after the accident. I remember lying there in Memphis thinking, Why did this happen? Did I do something wrong?

But two years later, I had managed to banish all thoughts of Why Me? I knew that God doesn't punish people for things they do. It doesn't work that way.

I'd think of all the adorable little kids with cancer or those who suffered abuse. They did nothing to deserve their fate. I knew there were people much worse off than I was and that I was so lucky in so many ways. We had great health insurance and excellent doctors and my family was so supportive. Still, as much as I tried to focus on the positive, some days I couldn't help feeling dejected. Karen used to say, "Wow, Hilary. You never get depressed."

But that was because I'd get buoyed up when people were around. The thing was, though, as the months wore on, people were visiting less and less. Some of my friends didn't even know about my latest surgeries. A lot of people assumed I was pretty much back to normal, and I don't blame them at all for going on with their lives.

I remember Holly going on vacation and feeling really guilty about it. But what was she supposed to do? Never go on vacation again?

When people did come to visit, naturally, they talked about their lives and told me stories about who they were seeing and what they were doing. But I could tell sometimes that my friends hesitated telling me about what they did that weekend or the night before, thinking they might make me feel left out.

Even Holly sometimes sat with me in near silence, afraid to tell me that she was on her way to get her hair highlighted or that she was expecting good news about a record deal, fearing it would make me feel bad.

Her clothing boutique, H. Audrey—named for our grandmother, who Holly resembles to a startling degree—was up and running by this time, and between hiring and buying for the store and recording songs for her new album, she was going full throttle. She wanted to tell me things, and I really wanted to hear it all, but it was a struggle for her not to feel bad and me not to feel envious. It was a no-win situation.

When people weren't around, my spirit had the potential to sink pretty low. On the upside, the painkillers weren't making me as nauseous as before, especially after the second or third month at home. The downside was that I was gaining weight; I must have put on twenty pounds. I was eating a lot of comfort food, mostly out of boredom. Then, my clothes didn't fit and that made me feel worse.

The whole surgery-recovery round robin seemed like a treadmill that I couldn't walk on very well and I couldn't get off.

But what else could I do? Per Karen's advice, I started taking cayenne pepper capsules again to help fight off infection and to help eliminate the bruising on my body. Then, every day, I'd sit up, grab onto the pulley above my bed, pull myself up, and swing my legs over the side of my bed. I'd flex my feet over and over, then I'd grab onto the walker and ease myself up, adjusting for the fact that my right leg was now shorter than my left due to the consolidation of the bone during the surgery.

So the weeks went by. One bled into another. But then, gradually, slowly, I began to notice that things were different. Could it be that during this round of therapy, things were just a little bit easier?

My left hip was healed. There was very little pain on that side anymore because the doctors had removed a part of my body that hurt with an artificial thing that had no sensation or nerve endings. My cracked ribs and broken tailbone were healed. My collarbone hadn't fully healed, but I could turn my neck and lift my arms in the air without a lot of pain. And even though when I first stood up, it felt like dozens of bees were stinging the bottoms of my feet, the sensation quickly went away. So just like that, there it was: a glimmer of hope.

After about three months or so, Dr. Kregor gave the nod for me to work out in the gym. In fact, he encouraged me to do so. He would push me by saying, "You don't have to always walk with a cane, Hilary." Sometimes, I'd get kind of mad at him. I mean, he was the guy who told me initially that walking without a cane was an ambitious goal. But then I caught on that he was just trying to challenge me. And it worked.

The first few times I lifted weights, I worked with Karen. Then, I worked with Dawn, another trainer at Athena. At first, I just did some free weights. Very light weights and very few reps. But I swear, almost immediately I could feel my body changing. When you start using certain muscle groups that have been idle for a while, the change is instant. It felt amazing.

After a couple of sessions, I started riding the stationary bike for a few minutes before I started my weight work. I also tried working out on the elliptical machine, but that was too challenging. My knees would get really weak and my legs would start burning like crazy. So I went back to the no-impact, sit-down comfort of the bike.

When I first started working out in the gym, people would ask me, are you sure it's okay for you to do that? Can't you hurt yourself? But putting weight on bones helps them heal and grow. As long as I took it slow and didn't push it, working out was an incredible boost for me. It still is.

People still ask me if it's okay for me to go to the gym. They also ask me if it's okay for me to do other things, like dancing, which I do occasionally, or wearing high heels, which I do but only rarely. I never really liked high shoes all that much. I'm tall enough as it is. But sometimes, you just want to wear a pair of heels. But I only wear platforms. Stilettos are a definite no-no.

People also ask me if I'm afraid the plate in my leg will break again. I try so hard not to think about it, but unfortunately, the thought crosses my mind. Last fall, I started having a lot of pain in my leg and it scared me. But I had been traveling; I took back-to-back trips to Dallas and Chicago and did a lot of walking. So when I came back, I went for an X-ray and was relieved to learn that the pain was caused by regular, everyday sore muscles.

With every passing month, things have gotten progressively stronger and the possibility of a break becomes less and less of a worry. I've had check-ups and bone density tests, and I've taken vitamins and Vitamin D shots. Everything feels solid. At this point, I truly believe that my plate won't break.

With major issues behind me, I had time to address things I'd been putting off, such as going to the dentist and the eye doctor. I was more than a little tired of visiting doctor's offices, but we scheduled one more visit, to see Dr. Burton Elrod, the team physician for the Tennessee Titans, so he could check my knees and collarbone. Both were healing on their own.

When a doctor told me good news like this, it always took a moment for it to sink in. At first, I didn't believe it. I would sit there for a while kind of waiting for the other shoe to drop. Then, when it didn't, I would grab my cane and walk out of there as fast as I could, grinning all the way. I'm sure the other people in the waiting room wondered what was up with the crazy girl with the cane hightailing it out of the doctor's office.

After my new plate had been in place for almost a year, I decided to take a trip with Melody to Isla Mujeres, Mexico, where her Dad was building a house.

Isla Mujeres, the easternmost point of Mexico, is such a cool place. It's a tiny island off Cancun. In fact, you fly into Cancun and take a ferry over the island. The island got its name, which in English means "Island of Women," because years ago, pirates and fishermen used to leave their women on the island for safe-keeping when they went off to pillage or fish or whatever they needed to do.

I didn't know if Isla Mujeres was still considered an island of women, but I did know that as far as my friend and I were concerned, this was an all girls' trip. Keven and I broke up in November. I truly believe that some people were meant to be just friends, so I'm happy to say that we still are. I really wasn't sad about out breakup. I was feeling optimistic for the first time in a long time and I was so looking forward to getting away.

First of all, it was January and we were going somewhere warm and sunny. Here was my chance to honor my vision—the one I'd clung to in the hospital—of a beach and a bucket of cold Coronas. Secondly, as I packed for the trip, it dawned on me that I would be baring a lot of skin in public for the first time in months. True, following the accident I wore my bathing suit every time I went to the pool for therapy. But usually, it was just me and Karen in the pool, or maybe a handful of other people in and out of the locker room who pretty much kept to themselves. I'd gone to my dad's beach house in Apalachicola the year before, but there was just a few of us there.

So as I put my tank tops, sundresses, and bathing suits in the bag, I hesitated for a minute and wondered how it would feel to be lying on the beach full of people, including guys, that is, if the Island of Women name turned out to be inaccurate. I looked down at the scars on my body: the big bump where my skin flap was attached, the marks where the skin grafts were scraped from my behind, the big white patch on my stomach—where did that come from?

Then I had the most amazing, welcome realization that I would ever have: I didn't care. I really didn't care what my body looked like or who saw it or what they thought about it or what they might say about it.

I never thought I would be secure enough in my own skin to feel this way. Like most women, I'd spent years criticizing my body. Look at my stomach! I was born with a gut. My thighs are huge. But that day, there was some sort of shift. It sounds trite, but I was happy to be alive, and that dominated everything. I felt truly free.

Later that week, when we were on the beach, we met a lot of different people, and sometimes, when they saw me with my cane, they asked me what happened. For the most part, this was just straightforward curiosity, similar to what you might say to someone who had a cast on her arm. The questions really didn't offend me, although there was one guy, an attorney from Texas, who would not let up and offered to represent me if I wanted to sue. (Sue? Sue who?)

At that point, I was getting a little tired of telling the story—especially the long version. So one day, I wrapped an ace bandage around my leg, thinking it would hide the scars and end the curiosity. But it backfired. The bandage only called attention to my leg. I got more questions than ever.

So I took off the bandage, and the rest of the week, I just relaxed. We hung out at our hotel, the Ixchel Beach Hotel, named for the Mayan goddess of love, fertility, and the moon, then later we drove our golf cart down to the private beach and looked out at the amazing view. I took a deep breath and just enjoyed being in a magical place, complete with the remains of a Mayan temple and ocean all around. At that point, if anyone asked me, "What happened?" I'd cover my eyes to shade them from the sun, look up at them and say, "Oh, I was in an accident. But I'm better now."

Then I'd leave it at that.

Over the next couple of months, I really didn't want to talk about the accident or bone grafts or plates or X-rays. What I really wanted to do was go out. So when my friends Kylie and Susan invited me to go with them to the Kentucky Derby in May, well, they didn't have to ask me twice.

This was the perfect getaway for me. Louisville is only a couple hours' drive from Nashville, and even though I knew mighty little about thoroughbred horse racing, I did know something about the most important part of the event: hats.

I love hats; I wear them a lot and I have a pretty good collection, but I knew I'd need something special and really over-the-top to wear to the Derby. So I went out shopping at Marshalls and found a French designer hat marked down from $500 to $200. This thing was huge, with long, black, rhinestone-tipped feathers and an enormous bow.

We had a blast. When we got to Churchill Downs, we ran into Bobby, who got us into the box seats on Turf Terrace. We saw all kinds of celebrities, including Kim Kardashian, Brooke Shields, and Paris Hilton, who were all decked out, wearing gorgeous gowns and hats. We saw Tom Brady and Eli Manning and took pictures with them.

Even though the main event, the one-and-a-quarter mile "Run for the Roses" only lasts two minutes, there are actually races going on all day long while people in the infield are picnicking, tossing Frisbees around, and drinking mint juleps.

I didn't bet on any races, mostly because I didn't understand what you were supposed to do. I assumed you had to bet hundreds or thousands of dollars, but I learned later you could bet $5 if you wanted to.

Susan bet on the race, picking a horse named Mine That Bird because he had the word "mine" in his name and her ex owns coal mines in Kentucky. She didn't care that the horse was a 50–1 long shot. She just liked the name.

Then, we all screamed when Mine That Bird won the race for the second biggest upset in Derby history. I'm definitely betting next time around.

I knew I was feeling better when I not only felt like going out but I was even game enough to go to one of my half-brother, Shelton's, shows. I saw Shelton, who is better known to his fans as Hank III (or just "3"), not long ago at The End, a funky club off Elliston Place in Nashville.

The End is one of those small venues that looks like the dark, unfinished basement of somebody's house, where people pack in and bands play really loud. That night I made sure to stand by the door in case the moshing got to be too much for me and I had to make a quick getaway.

Whether he's playing at The End or a big theater, Shelton is one of the most distinctive performers on the planet. During his shows, he starts out with a set of country songs, then halfway through he switches to hard core punk. It's outrageous.

And his audience is even more outrageous, or I should say, diverse. At the show I saw at The End, there was a kid standing next to me with a two-foot, bright orange Mohawk. On the other side of him, there was a forty-year-old guy in a business suit. Then there were a few grandmothers sitting on stools in the back—obvious Hank Williams fans.

According to Shelton, he does the country stuff first because he can't scream and then switch to singing. Makes sense: Sing, then scream.

Shelton knows that a lot of people in the audience leave during his second set. (I admit to sometimes being one of them.) So I think maybe he structures his show that way out of consideration for the fans who just like the country stuff. In an odd way, he's being polite.

And despite his rebel image, Shelton is polite. He's also the spitting image of my grandfather, which makes him proud but also makes him crazy because people bring it up constantly. Every time someone writes a story about my brother, they always mention Minnie Pearl and her now-famous comment she made the first time she ever saw Shelton: "Lord, honey. You're a ghost!"

According to Shelton, Minnie actually did say that, and surprisingly, he also says that it didn't tick him off. In fact, he really liked Minnie. She was a good friend of my grandfather's, and Shelton loved hearing Minnie's stories. Before she died, they used to go to lunch all the time. Shelton says that Minnie was also friends with his mother, Gwen, who was my dad's second wife. Gwen and Dad divorced when Shelton was three years old, so we have a lot in common. Neither of us saw Dad a whole lot growing up.

Shelton and I would see each other from time to time, though. In fact, our mothers became friendly when we were little, so he would come over and play with me and Holly. I remember him riding his skateboard when he was around thirteen or fourteen years old. He was really good at it, and because I was only six or seven years old at the time, I was in awe watching him skate down steps and do flips and tricks.

When we were teenagers, Mom had choir practice on Sunday afternoons, so Holly and I would sometimes spend part of the day with Gwen and her husband and Shelton, if he was around. These were the years when Shelton wore a Mohawk and chains around his boots and wrists. His mom made him go to Christ Church, where we went, and sometimes I'd see him sitting behind us, a few rows back by himself. Shelton was going through a rough time then. Although we never talked about it, I know he was angry, partially at Dad. He was moody and quiet, but he was always super nice to me.

For as long as I can remember, Shelton played music. He played all kinds of instruments, but he was great on the drums, and when he was growing up, he played in a lot of different bands. He even played with Dad's band a few times, but mostly, punk rock was his genre of choice.

When he was younger, I don't think Shelton ever seriously considered cashing in on his name or playing country music, certainly not commercial country music. But then in 1995 he was hit with a paternity suit.

Out of the blue, he found out he had a three-year-old son and owed $24,000 in back child support. He would also be required to keep up future payments, so at age twenty-two, Shelton had to find a way to boost his income immediately.

He started calling himself Hank III and took to the stage in Branson, Missouri, dressed like my grandfather and singing his songs. It's weird to think of Shelton doing exactly what my Dad did years earlier when he started his career: mimicking my grandfather. But that's what he did.

Then in 1996 he made a deal with Curb Records to make a record called *Three Hanks*, in which he and Dad would add vocals to old Hank Williams recordings. It's wild what studio technology can do today. They digitally separated my grandfather's vocals from the old tracks and new musicians played the songs to new tracks recorded by Dad and Shelton.

It's a very cool record, but I think Shelton was a little embarrassed that he did it. He wasn't ashamed of singing Hank Williams songs or doing something with Dad, although the two of them were far from close at the time. Rather, he just felt pushed into it, as if it were really early in his career to be doing something like this. He didn't feel like he was being himself.

These days, however, nobody can accuse Shelton of not being himself. If you squint, you might see my grandfather, but if you open your eyes wide, you see that under his cowboy hat, the sides of his head are shaved and there is a two-foot-long braid cascading down his back. He might be wearing a western-looking shirt, but more than likely the sleeves are cut off and he's got a "F——— Curb" T-shirt on underneath it.

You should see the band house he rents with a couple of friends in east Nashville. They call it "The Haunted Ranch," and a couple of years ago, I made the mistake of telling him I would stay there and dogsit for him for a couple of days.

I thought maybe they called it the Haunted Ranch because it sits on top of this hill and it's really dark and wild looking, with skulls all over the place and huge bandannas covering the windows and gig posters and hats that fans threw on stage covering the walls. I didn't think it was really haunted.

But one night I got a flashlight and took his three German Shepherds outside, and when we came back in, they kept barking and jumping all around. Dogs can sense things, and it made me nervous. Then a chill went up my spine when I was sitting there by myself, and I heard the sound of a baby crying. There was no baby anywhere near that house. Later, my friend Bobby Tomberlin came over and went into the bathroom, where he heard a man laughing. It was a really deep, low-sounding laugh. And we were the only ones there.

The Haunted Ranch is just one of many inspirations for Shelton's music, which is a wild, Jekyll-and-Hyde mix of half-neotraditional country, half-hardcore punk-metal, which people refer to as cowpunk or hellbilly. Songs such as "Trashville" or "Dick in Dixie" or the above-mentioned Curb T-shirt leave no doubt about how Shelton views the Nashville establishment.

Shelton makes his opinions known. A few years back, he was invited to play a big anniversary show at the Grand Ole Opry. When he came onstage, he said, "Well, folks, here's your big fiftieth anniversary, and [Hank Williams] is not a member. Don't you think it's about time to change that?"

As country music fans know, the first Hank was kicked off the Opry a few months before he died. Everybody, including Shelton, knows that the Opry had no choice but to fire him back then. But what about now? The Opry uses his image and makes money off some of his Opry recordings, so Shelton and a lot of other people think it would be appropriate to make him a member again.

To make his point, Shelton wrote a song, "The Grand Ole Opry Ain't So Grand," which is on his 2008 album, *Damn Right, Rebel Proud.* He has also been very vocal and supportive of the grassroots movement to reinstate Hank Williams into the Opry (reinstatehank.org).

The Opry would have to make a big exception to put my grandfather back on its rolls because, currently, no deceased members are on the roster. But how cool would it be if they reinstated all the great members—like Johnny Cash, Porter Waggoner, and Patsy Cline—who have passed away? It would be great for the Opry and it would mean a lot to the family and fans of Hank Williams. So who knows? Maybe we'll see that happen sometime soon.

The last time I saw Shelton was at Chris and Holly's wedding back in October of 2009. Actually, I saw him a couple weeks before that, too, when I ran into him at one of the live music clubs on lower Broadway. Later that night, he dropped me off at Melody's house (actually, her boyfriend, Gary's, house), where I'd left my dog Sophie, my little Maltese poodle. It was late, so I decided to crash on their couch. Then, in the middle of the night, I got up to go to the bathroom.

At Gary and Melody's house, there is a hallway with two doors, side-by-side. One door opens to the bathroom. The other door opens to a steep staircase that leads into the basement.

Guess which door I opened?

By mistake, I opened the door to the basement, took a step, and went tumbling down the stairs. When I got up from my crumpled heap, I realized I had broken my arm. So much for relegating all my broken bones to my lower half. Now, with Holly's wedding just two weeks away, my arm was in a cast.

And poor Mom! Because I broke my left arm, the one I used to hold my cane, she had to come and stay with me for the next couple weeks to help me get around.

It was a little bit challenging performing my maid of honor duties while wearing a cast. I thought the toughest part of the ceremony for me would be standing for thirty minutes. But as it turned out, holding two bouquets—both Holly's and mine—while she said her vows was the hardest part. My arm was killing me. At least no one could see my cast. I covered it with a wrap that I special ordered to match my black Vera Wang maid of honor dress.

The ceremony itself was absolutely beautiful. It had been pouring buckets in Nashville for three weeks, so Holly was really worried. She had planned for everything to take place outside and had no backup plan. Then, as if on cue, on the day of the wedding, the sun burst out through the clouds.

Both the ceremony and reception were at Cedarwood Mansion, an elegant 1830s farm estate with a big, shady lawn and roses around the terrace. Holly planned the whole wedding by herself, putting it all together in just over two months.

It was so gorgeous. She brought in a lot of things herself, including this cool, old wooden chandelier with votive candles that they hung up above the wedding cake. They set up antique pews on the lawn for the guests and put up three antique windows from the Ryman Auditorium, the original site of the Grand Ole Opry, as the backdrop for the bride and groom.

The afternoon of the wedding, we were getting our hair and makeup done when Holly called our friend Rhett. "Hey, Rhett," she said. "Can you do me a favor and swing by my loft on your way over here?"

"What did you forget?" Rhett asked.

"My dress." Then she starts describing where the dress is hanging. "Okay, just go in my bedroom and on the back of the door . . ."

"Holly," Rhett said. "I think I can find a twelve-foot-long wedding gown."

The reception was so much fun, with the R&B band playing and everybody dancing and the videographer making a cool, retro vintage film with an 8mm camera. At one point, Holly got up and sang "Signed, Sealed, Delivered" with the band. Then she and Chris danced to that Mark Knopfler and Emmylou Harris song "I Dug up a Diamond."

Bobby (a.k.a. Kid Rock) was there and got up and sang a couple of songs. He was so sweet to everybody; he stayed the whole time and must have posed for a picture with every single guest at the wedding.

Dad didn't stay as long as Bobby; he left right after we took pictures. He doesn't do well in crowds. He's kind of legendary in our family for his short goodbyes, but I was proud of him for staying as long as he did.

I was even more proud of him and Mom for welcoming Chris into our family. Both of them had concerns prior to the wedding—not about Chris, who everybody likes, but about typical "I'm worried about my daughter" stuff. Mom was worried that Holly and Chris were getting married too fast. Although they had been friends for many years—we all had—they'd only been dating a few months when they decided to get married. Chris is a great drummer and guitar player and has worked as Holly's tour manager. And recently, Chris got the gig as the silent fifth member of Kings of Leon. But Mom worried about Holly marrying a musician. After all, she's been there.

And Dad? He was worried about Holly marrying a musician because he is one.

But everybody talked it out. Mom and Holly and Chris even talked to a counselor together before the wedding, and Mom came away feeling convinced that Holly and Chris were right for each other.

Since the wedding, they've been on several tours together, with Chris playing guitar for Holly at shows in Europe and at home. And that's just the beginning of their story.

Chapter 14

Good Sounds and Great Vibes

I'm sitting in a small, dark, soundproof room, with the heavy door pulled shut and locked tight. The room has a darkened window on one side, where I can see out but no one can see in unless they put their face right up to the glass.

It makes me feel safe.

The gray, granite walls and the octagonal shape of the room, which is actually part of producer Matt Wilder's recording studio, remind me of the top of a castle tower. So I can't help it. Today, I feel a little bit like a princess.

But so far, there's no sign of Prince Charming. It's just me, sitting in the dark—except for a flickering candle—in front of a vintage microphone with my headphones on, listening to instructions from Matt, who is sitting in front of the soundboards in another room. "Okay, Hilary," Matt says, "Why don't you sing it through once so I can get a level for you and you can get warmed up . . . "

We already decided to do the vocals line by line, meaning I'd sing one or two lines of a song over and over before moving on to the next couple of lines. He planned to save all the takes on his computer, which looks like a heart rate monitor with all the lines moving up and down. Later, he would pick the best one of each, the take he likes the best, and digitally cut them into the final version of the song.

"Ready?" Matt says. "Okay, from the verse. Try to get it right in the pocket."

I've always loved being in recording studios. I remember going into Emerald Studios with my dad when I was little and he was recording "Hey, Good Lookin'" with Reba McEntire. Back then, she was Reba with the big hair and was so sweet and friendly. Right when we walked in, she motioned me over to where she was sitting in the sound engineer's chair and said, "Honey! Come sit in my lap!"

So I did. We all listened to a playback of the song, then she let me play with some of the buttons and move the sliders up and down the board.

Today, the recording process is vastly different than it was when Dad was making records in the 1980s. And back in my grandfather's day, records were made with the band playing into one or two mics. There were no separate tracks. They played the song all the way through each time. If somebody messed up, they had to start all over again.

Now, everything is done digitally.

In the days of analog tape, the engineer or producer would only have twenty-four tracks to work with, so if he used up twenty-one of them on the instrumental part of the song and wanted to use more than three for vocals, he would have to erase something. Today, you have an almost unlimited number of takes.

As much as the technology has changed, however, the structure of most recording studios has pretty much stayed the same. Although Matt's studio has its own unique vibe, with an under-the-sea ocean mural painted on the stairway walls and a Kandinskylike pink and orange sunburst splatter painted on the ceiling, like most studios, the walls are covered with rectangular-shaped foam panels that look like modern sculpture. But these oversized sponges have a purpose. They aren't there just for decoration. They are put there to absorb the sound.

The rooms in recording studios are built in such a way that there are no parallel surfaces. That's why my little castle room is shaped like an octagon. The sound literally has to bounce off the walls.

And as far as sound goes, nothing is more crucial than the all-important microphone. Many producers like to use an original U47, the first-ever condenser mic that was introduced in 1947 and, as many people believe, has never been improved upon. The Beatles used one of these on *Abbey Road* and Faith Hill used one on *Breathe*.

So I guess the ol' U47 is good enough for me.

It's cool to be combining the old with the new. The vintage mic flatters your voice, and the popper stopper, the little piece of material stretched out in front of it, muffles the "p's" so they don't pop so much. Then the digital technology captures the character of the sound. Perfect.

That day in the studio, we were working on the vocal part of a demo. The studio musicians had worked on their parts earlier in the week. Although they were in different rooms—the drummer in one room, the bass and guitar player in another—they played each take of the song together while the producer talked to them through their headphones. The song we were recording, "World Without Hope," is a beautiful song written by Blu Sanders about bringing hope to the world by lending a helping hand.

Blu is a great singer-songwriter. He has made several albums and plays with the Eli Young band a lot. He and I have written together before. In fact, we cowrote "Sign of Life," my song about my accident and recovery.

People often ask me if I wrote songs while I was in the hospital or at home during recovery. For the most part, the answer is no. Mostly I listened to music, usually something like Coldplay or anything that felt soothing or healing. I'd pop my earphones in and tune out the world.

It's hard to relate to, I know, but so many of my days were consumed with just breathing and existing and numbing pain and trying to sleep. I didn't even read much—not books anyway. Sometimes I'd flip through magazines, something fun like *People* or *InStyle*. But for months, I hardly read at all. I just didn't have the energy.

But one day during the first summer I was at home recovering, Blu came over to work on a song with me. Angela, who was his roommate, thought we would work well together and that it would be good for me to try to write. Karen kept saying the same thing. "There's nothing wrong with your hands, Hilary!" Karen said. "There's nothing wrong with your brain."

So Blu came over to work on a song. As I was still in my hospital bed in Mom's living room, Blu pulled up a chair next to me and brought out his guitar. I told him some of the details of the accident. Then we talked about pain and hurting and healing and how I felt a sense of hope for the first time when Dr. Croce said, "Pain is a sign of life."

"That's a great idea for a song," Blu said.

So, I wrote down a few lines:

A Wednesday, a Memphis sun
I saw a prophet on Highway 61 . . .

I kept jotting phrases, describing what happened (*and there was silence*) and who was there (*a preacher and a family man*) and what the scene looked like (*the broken glass, the twisted steel*).

Blu kept asking me questions and I'd write another line. Then he started working on the melody and tossed out ideas for other lyrics as we went along.

I love the phrase we came up with for the PolyHeme: *a tiny miracle, made of other's hands.*

By the end of the afternoon, we'd finished the song. I sang it through a couple of times, softly. Then I tucked it away.

Some of the same friends who were encouraging me to write songs during my recovery were also trying to convince me to play some shows, even when I was still in my wheelchair.

I thought about it. I mean, it could have worked in my favor. Who's going to be rude and talk during your set if you came out in a wheelchair? But, in the end, I just couldn't bring myself to do it. I thought I'd look pitiful, and the idea of figuring out how to get on and off a stage was a nightmare to me. Besides, until it was fully healed, I couldn't really rest a guitar on my femur without grimacing.

But in the summer of 2009, I was ready. The wheelchair was in mothballs. The crutches were tucked away in a closet. I was still using a cane part of the time, but I knew if I pushed it, I could walk out on a stage without it, get up on a stool, and sing. That's what I was waiting for. The perfect opportunity came when Shawn Carnes invited me to participate in his *Familiar Faces* acoustic showcase at 12th and Porter.

Showcases go on all the time in Nashville. Sometimes, they'll consist of one singer or a band performing for a few record company execs in hopes of getting a record deal or a new band will perform for a few journalists. Those types of shows are kind of tense because, instead of a real audience, the band is playing to a small, jaded, nondrinking, and usually unresponsive cluster of people. The worst is when it's just you and a couple of poker-faced record company people who keep their hands in their laps as you play in a brightly lit conference room.

A showcase like the one Shawn organized, which would feature eight or ten singer-songwriters, is much better for the performers because it's a real show in a real club with a real audience and a full bar.

It's great for music fans, too. On any given night in Nashville, you can stumble into a show like this one, pay little or no cover charge, and see incredible talent like Nathan Barlowe, the songwriter and lead singer for Luna Halo or his brother Cary Barlowe, who has written songs for Taylor Swift and Lady Antebellum and won a Grammy for the TobyMac song "Made to Love." Sometimes, you'll even get to see someone on the caliber of Bekka Bramlett, Stevie Nicks's replacement as Fleetwood Mac's lead singer from 1993 to 1995, who was closing the show that night.

I thought I'd be anything but sleepy the night before the show, but around 10:00, I was lying in bed watching a rerun of *Keeping Up with the Kardashians* on TV when I started nodding off. But then I made myself get up to take Sophie outside. The minute I pushed myself out of bed, she bounded off the couch and started whimpering and jumping wildly in front of the door.

"Hold on!" I said, reaching for her leash and bending down to clip it to her collar. I took the leash in my left hand and opened the front door with my right, propping it open with my hip. Then I reached for one of my canes that I keep in the umbrella stand by the front door and followed Sophie, who was already halfway down the corridor. I tried not to choke her or drop my keys as she ran ahead of me and down the front steps. I let her pee in the grass, then we came right back inside. She scampered across the floor and I immediately climbed back into bed.

After my head hit the pillow, I was asleep almost immediately. I could wait until morning to worry about the songs and what I was going to wear and all the people who were coming to see me and the people I forgot to invite . . .

Morning came earlier than I expected. I woke up around 6:30 a.m. when I heard my phone beeping. I picked it up and read the text message, BREAKFAST?

Dad was in town, and as always, he was up early. "This'll be a great start to your day!" he said when I called him back. "Your send-off breakfast!"

I was excited to see him, so I splashed water on my face, quickly got dressed, and went to pick him up at Bobby's condo, where Dad usually stays when he's in Nashville.

People probably wouldn't expect this, but Bobby's condo is in a very elegant, high-end neighborhood in a very traditional, historical-looking building. But that's on the outside. Inside, it's all Kid Rock, with each of the three levels reflecting the different genres of music he plays.

The first floor has a rock-and-roll theme, complete with a big picture of Jimi Hendrix made from license plates. The second floor is all country, with leather couches and cowhide pillows trimmed with tassels and a very cool, retro-looking painting of Hank Williams. The third floor is the hip-hop level, where Bobby's bedroom (with antique mirrors on the ceiling) and the guest rooms are located.

Dad always stays in one of the guest rooms, although it's hard to picture him getting any sleep in a bright orange room with a Technicolor bedspread.

Bobby's condo is only two minutes away from my place, so I got there pretty fast. "There's my Nashville chauffeur!" Dad said, as he climbed into the passenger seat and leaned over to kiss my cheek.

I smiled at him as we drove down Harding Avenue past Belle Meade Mansion to Le Peep, a sweet, kind of trendy diner bustling with people and filled with the smell of bacon and freshly baked bread. As we walked in, a man at one of the tables looked up at us and started doing really loud duck calls. My dad cracked up and went over to shake the guy's hand. It was Norro Wilson, one of Kenny Chesney's producers and, evidently, a fellow hunter. "I knew this guy when he was just a little kid," Norro told me, pointing at Dad with his fork.

We had the best breakfast. Dad ordered Huevos Rancheros. The plate was huge. He was very excited that they had that on the menu. I had Eggs Florentine, which really filled me up, and as soon as we finished, I felt like I needed a nap.

Before I took Dad back to Bobby's condo, where his assistant was due to pick him up and drive him home to Paris, Tennessee, we stopped by Holly's condo. Katie was staying there all week while she was taking acting classes in town, and Dad wanted to give her a check to pay for the classes.

I swear Katie is going to be famous some day. She has done some modeling and she photographs beautifully. She's also an amazing basketball player, which, as I recently found out, was also my grandmother Audrey's favorite sport to play. But acting is Katie's real calling.

She is so brave. One night when she came back from a class, she met me over at a friend's house where a bunch of us were eating dinner. After only a little prodding, she got up and did the monologue she learned in the class, an intense scene about a troubled teenager, right in front of everybody.

Anyway, we dropped off the check in the mailbox because it was so early and Katie would no doubt still be asleep. Then we drove to my condo. I had just moved in and Dad hadn't seen the place yet. When he walked in, he looked all around and whistled loud, "Wheeeeeeew! This is great. Check out this fireplace. Your old place looks like a barn compared to this!"

After I dropped off Dad back at Bobby's, I went home and took a nap—and once again, had no trouble falling asleep. When I got up, I still felt lethargic. My allergies were really bothering me and I needed some quick energy. So, I called my friend Trish Vogel, who had offered the night before to come over and give me a B-12 shot.

Trish is one of the coolest people I know. She's a little older than me, although I'm not at liberty to disclose exactly how much older. She's tall, blonde, and beautiful, but with Trish, it's much more than looks. She is a whirlwind of energy and upbeat attitude. She does all this stuff—acting, singing, radio hosting, writing— and lives in L.A. now. But luckily for me, she was in town the day of my show.

I've never seen someone travel so light and as efficiently as Trish. Once, on a trip to Key West for a wedding, Trish brought a tiny carry-on bag packed with a ball gown, a bathing suit, and a pair of shorts. So when she showed up that morning, she had a small purse packed with everything she needed to give me my shot, including rubbing alcohol and cotton balls. I mean, who carries that kind of stuff in her purse?

Then, after I mentioned that my allergies were acting up and my throat was a little sore, she went into the kitchen, got a spoon, and came at me with it, ordering, "Stick out your tongue so I can look at your throat!"

Trish left just as Jessica Langer, my backup singer, and Dan Hoisington, my guitar player, were walking in. "Nurse Betty, at your service!" Trish said, waving at them.

"Is she really a nurse?" Jessica said.

"No," I said. "That's just Auntie Mame."

I met Jessica and Dan through my friend Laurie Webb, who is another ball of energy (I must subconsciously seek out these types). She is a fantastic singer who used to play in the band

Lollievox. Leann Rimes cut one of her songs, "You Are." I love Laurie's music and she does all genres—pop, dance stuff, jazz. We knew each other for a long time but really only connected a few years ago during a Christmas party at Quad, a popular Nashville recording studio.

Musicians always make the rounds at the cool Christmas parties, mostly because we can eat and drink for free. I knew some people there and was having fun, but sometimes it's painful for me to make small talk, so I went over and started playing the piano, when Laurie came over, sat down, and listened to me play.

We talked for a long time and just really hit it off. Soon after that, we started writing songs together and just really clicked. We wrote one song called, "Let Love Speak," which is a little depressing because we were both brokenhearted at the time. The next time we got together we said, "No more sad songs!" So we wrote a song called "Burning Up the Night," a fun, wild, party song. Then we wrote "Either Way," a song I love that Merle Kilgore used to play for people. He'd go around saying, "You need to hear this song! It's a hit!"

When Laurie and I get together, we end up talking a lot. She tells me stuff about her daughter or her boyfriend.

When you're a songwriter, technically, you're working even when you're just talking because you never know where your next good idea will come from. One day we were talking about our dads and Laurie told me about how she grew up traveling with her father. They would actually explore the places James Michener wrote about, using his books as a guide. Once, they took off for several months and traveled all around Hawaii. I tried to imagine spending time with my dad like that—one-on-one time, just the two of us.

Laurie and I haven't written that song yet.

It's hard for me to write really personal stuff, to lay it all out there for everybody to hear. But I guess I'd better get used to it.

After all, later that night, I'd be singing a song about the transformation of my entire life.

With just a few hours until showtime, we got to work. Dan put his guitar on his lap and Jessica started jotting notes on a legal pad. "How do you want to end this?" asked Jessica, as she hummed the chorus of "West Hollywood Monday Mornings," the first song of the four-song set we'd be playing. "Let's go through the chords before the instrumental . . . "

I was relieved that they both knew the songs so well; they learned them the week before just by listening to them a few times on a laptop. I thought they both sounded great and I liked Jessica's voice with mine. I started to relax a little bit.

After playing the first three songs a couple of times, we were ready to run through "Sign of Life."

"So, do you guys think we're ending on a downer?" I asked.

"Not at all," said Jessica. "I really think it's going to be powerful."

"I like this weird jazzy chord," said Dan. "It sounds kind of like Coldplay."

Then I looked at my phone, which had been beeping nonstop with messages, and realized we had twenty minutes to get to the rehearsal.

I hadn't been to 12th and Porter for a while, but I knew they'd been doing all kinds of improvements in the larger of the two performing rooms. They installed a new lighting system and the stage looked bigger and more impressive than I remembered. But as we walked in, none of the spotlights were on. Instead, the stage was bathed in candlelight. Several tall candelabras were set up around the microphones and three stools at center stage. It was gorgeous. It absolutely took my breath away.

At that point, one of the technicians walked by and I heard him say, "Thirty grand in new lights and they're using candles."

I loved it.

This looked so much better than the last place I'd played before the accident, a low-end place called The Muse over by the big adult bookstore near the I-40 ramp downtown. I remember that night vividly because the sound kept going out. On a positive note, I played "Let Somebody Save Me" during my set, a song I'm really proud of that I wrote with John Paul White and Kris Bergenes. People in the audience were actually crying.

"So, Hilary, let's run through it once for sound," Shawn said.

I nodded and started walking toward the stage. I was using my cane and walking pretty well, but then I stopped. The stage was about two feet off the floor. I had no idea how I would get up there.

Maybe I needed some dancers to lift me. I could wear long gloves and stretch out my arms like Marilyn Monroe did in "Diamonds Are a Girl's Best Friend." But then Shawn and Dan each took one of my arms and I took the big step up to the stage. I set my cane on the ground, sat down on the stool, and adjusted the mic so it was high enough for me.

Then, looking out into the dark room that was empty except for the shadow of the sound guy, a few other techs, and the film crew, I sang "Sign of Life" twice. It was kind of awkward singing into the air—kind of spooky, with just me, Jessica, and Dan, and with the candles flickering away.

When I was finished, I walked backstage and through the hallway into the lounge. A cameraman and the local Fox entertainment reporter, Stacy McCloud, were waiting for me to do an interview for the 6:00 and 11:00 news that night, so I joined them and sat down on a big, puffy red couch to do the interview. This was the first chance I'd had all day to be nervous, and my stomach did a couple of pronounced backflips.

I really don't like talking on camera, but Stacy was really nice and friendly. Once she started asking questions, it was like talking to a friend. As I told the story of the accident and all my surgeries, I noticed Stacy's eyes growing wide. This is so much a part of my life now that I forget how shocked people are when they hear the details. Sometimes I suspect that people think I'm exaggerating or making things up.

Later, when they aired the piece on the news, they flashed pictures of the mangled truck and an incredibly unflattering shot of me in my hospital bed. After that, I figured the show should be a breeze.

I've heard many singers, some of them big, big stars, say that it's much scarier playing for a small audience than performing a show for a huge crowd. I agree. I'd be less intimidated playing for twenty thousand people in a stadium than I would for twenty people at a party.

Smaller rooms are scary because you can see faces and hear comments. And sometimes the audience can even see your hands shake.

Probably the most intimidating performance I've ever done was a few years back when Holly and I sang at Dad's induction into the Songwriter's Hall of Fame in Nashville. It was a small crowd that night, which in itself is scary enough. It was a really fancy gala event, and it seemed as if every important person in the music business was there. Holly made the speech introducing Dad, and even though she's usually at ease in these situations, she was terrified. She says she has never been more nervous than she was talking to those people that night.

Singing is definitely easier than talking, but you can't imagine what it's like to be looking at the faces of all the record company presidents and agents and producers—all the bigwigs in town. And just for added pressure, I was walking with one crutch under my arm, praying I wouldn't trip while walking up the steps.

Well, Holly did great. Then, after the speech, she sang "Feelin' Better." Then I came up and—thank God I didn't fall—we surprised Dad and sang "Blues Man," the beautiful song he wrote about Mom when I was a baby. I love that song and I think we did well, with Holly taking one verse, then me taking another.

I'll never forget singing that song. Of all the people in the room, for some reason, my eyes locked on Jimmy Buffet, who stared at me the entire time from his seat in the front row. Maybe it was just me, but I thought he looked way too intense for a guy who has made a living being laid back.

So being a small venue, 12th and Porter fit my definition of scary. The place was pretty much full; I'm guessing there were around two hundred people there when I got to the club.

Earlier that week, I'd put a notice about the showcase on MySpace and Facebook and texted everyone I could think of to invite them. So many of my friends and family showed up that night. I couldn't believe it.

It was around 7:45 when I arrived, and because I was due to go on at 8:15, I immediately went through the kitchen and up the back stairs to the green room (which is not green) to wait until we went on. Dan and Jessica were there, watching the show through the backstage window. We were talking and laughing. People were coming in and out of the room. Then I noticed it was 8:30. Then it was 9:00. I kept getting text messages, "When are you going on?" and "What's up?"

I didn't know what to tell people. I guess they'd started a little late and some of the earlier acts were playing extra songs. Although I felt bad that some of my friends were waiting so long—it got to be 9:30, then 10:00 . . . —the good thing was that we sat around so long that my nerves began to wear off.

It was like hanging out at the swimming pool when you're a kid and waiting in a really long line to jump off the high dive. You're scared when you first get in the line. But it moves really slowly, and after watching one person after another slowly climb the ladder, jump off, land in the water, and not get hurt, you stop feeling scared—until it's your turn.

"Okay, Hilary, you're on . . . "

Jessica walked down the stairs first and I followed behind her, using my cane. Dan walked behind us carrying his guitar. We made our way through the kitchen, where waiters were hustling in and out, picking up plates of food, and stacking dishes into bus trays. We walked down the hall and stood just out of sight at stage left.

"Ladies and gentlemen, Hilary Williams!"

As the crowd let out a big, loving whoop, I took a deep breath and hesitated for just a moment. Then I stashed my cane in the corner and walked out onstage. Everybody was cheering. That noise, filled with so many voices I knew and loved, was something I'll never forget.

Despite my fears about the small room, I really couldn't make out many faces. Unlike rehearsal, there were spotlights to augment the candles, so it was hard to see past the front row. One face I could see, though, was my mom's. She was sitting tall in her chair at a table, front and center, smiling and clapping wildly through my first couple of songs.

Then, she sat quietly as I began to sing my last song:

A Wednesday,
a Memphis sun . . .

Afterword

Would Hank Williams have become as famous as he did if he hadn't died so young?

I don't know the answer to that one.

What I do know is that life is the very greatest gift. I almost lost my life, and now that I've gotten it back, I want to live for a very long time.

So much trauma and sadness and loneliness have been passed down in my family, especially on the Williams side. I believe that it's time for it to stop.

My story ends here for now, four-and-a-half years after the terrible wreck that my sister and I survived.

On a very sad note, in March 2010 Cindy Parker (a.k.a. "Big Cindy"), one of the Life Flight nurses who saved my life, died in a helicopter crash. Big Cindy literally brought me back to life, and everyone who knew her is heartbroken that she is gone. Incredibly—but true to form—she lost her life while working to save others. I am so grateful to have known her.

I am also so grateful that after twenty-three surgeries, I was able to keep all my limbs, and that after a good bit of rearranging and adding and taking away certain things, my body is as close to normal as I could ever have hoped. I still have pain every day, but my goal is to not let it define me. The pain is manageable and worth it because it usually visits me after doing things I am so grateful to be able to do, such as walking or riding a bike or driving or standing.

This experience tested my faith and it thrills me to say that, spiritually, I've never felt better than I do now.

Time and again, during the months I was recovering, Mom would read certain Bible verses to me, which comfort me still. One of our favorites was Isaiah 53:4–5:

> Surely He has borne our griefs (sicknesses, weaknesses, and distresses) and carried our sorrows and pains, yet we (ignorantly) considered him stricken, smitten, and afflicted by God . . . But He was wounded for our transgressions, He was bruised for our guilt and iniquities; the chastisement (needed to obtain) peace and well-being for us was upon Him, and with the stripes (that wounded) Him we are healed and whole.

I'm ready. It's time to begin the rest of my life.